The Danger Is
Everywhere!

28 Dec 01

Merry,

Kellemes karácsony ünepeket

és

boldog új évet!

[signature]

The Danger Is Everywhere!

The Insecurity of Transition in Postsocialist Hungary

Barbara A. West

University of the Pacific

WAVELAND

PRESS, INC.

Prospect Heights, Illinois

For information about this book, contact:
Waveland Press, Inc.
P.O. Box 400
Prospect Heights, Illinois 60070
(847) 634-0081
www.waveland.com

Contents

Brief and Approximate Hungarian Pronunciation Guide

Hungarian is a fairly easy language for an English speaker to learn how to pronounce, my one saving grace considering how difficult its grammar and vocabulary are! Unlike in English, every letter is pronounced, even when the same letter is doubled, and for the most part every letter is pronounced the same in every word.

a as in caught

e, u are pronounced much like their short vowel sounds in English

i as in meet

o as in doe, sort of

á as in baa, the sound sheep make

é as in same

ö as in furl, sort of

ü as in view, sort of

í, ó, ú, ő, ű are pronounced much like their short versions, but longer

Many consonants are pronounced the same as in English, with a few exceptions. Where many English speakers have difficulty is with the consonant combinations.

c as in sits, even when it is the first letter in a word

cs as in church; ch in the name Szechényi is also pronounced this way

g as in guard

gy as in medium, sort of...

j and ly are pronounced the same, as in yellow

r should be rolled a bit, as it is in Spanish

s as in **sh**ort

sz as in **s**ame, do not pronounce the z! Szeged is pronounced Seged, with emphasis on the first syllable

zs as in plea**s**ure or A**s**ia

Acknowledgments

So many people have helped in the preparation of the many drafts of this manuscript that I can't begin to express my gratitude to all of them. I hope anyone I've left out will forgive me. I first have to thank my parents for supporting me in everything I do and visiting me everywhere I go. I also want to express my gratitude to the Anthropology Department at the University of Rochester, for getting me ready for my first field experience in a non-English speaking country, and to the SOAN Department at Colgate University for making me read dozens of Waveland Press ethnographies. I also owe a tremendous debt to everyone who made my fieldwork the exciting, challenging, and successful experience it was: Anci Néni, Andi, Anna, the Árva family, Attila, Blanka, Don, the Erdélyi family, Érika, Éva, the Fenyvesi family, Flóra, the Garamvölgyi family, the Hegyi family, Iluska Néni, Irén, Józsi Bacsi, Kati, Lajos, Marika Néni, Nusi, Péter, Sanyi (gone long before his time), Tamás, Tibor, Vali, Zoli, Zsuzsa, the Physical Anthropology Department at JATE, the Cultural Anthropology Department at ELTE, the women at Ópusztaszer, the staff of the Csongrád county museums, and countless other Hungarians who talked to me, answered my questions, and made me feel welcome. I also have to thank Michelle Landers for helping me get through my fieldwork. Without her encouragement to keep going with the language, help in everything from translations to shopping, and presence in Szeged I don't think I would have been able to write this book at all. Thank you to my dissertation committee at the University of Rochester, particularly to Ayala Emmett, for encouraging me to write the very first draft of what has become this book. The last stages of the production of this book owe a tremendous debt to many people as well. Dee Rubin encouraged me to continue on with the project after so many years away from it, and the School of International Studies at the University of the Pacific gave me the opportunity to do so. Ramesh Krishnamurthy drew the maps and scanned my photos, for which I owe him a great debt. Three University of the Pacific students, Dallas

Frohrib, Marian Hart, and Heather Torvend, read the entire manuscript and gave me extensive feedback. Fran Murphy has read every chapter at least three times and never seemed to tire of it. I can't thank her enough for her tireless support in this project and everything I do! Finally, thank you also to the two anonymous reviewers who helped me to clarify almost every argument I've made throughout the book, and, especially, to Tom Curtin and Don Rosso at Waveland Press. Tom's faith in me as an anthropologist, writer, and editor has been an inspiration; I hope he never regrets his decision. Don's editorial work has improved not only this book but my writing in general. I envy his skill with words. Of course, any remaining shortcomings are my own.

I would also like to acknowledge Taylor and Francis, PO Box 25, Abingdon, Oxfordshire, OX14 3UE, http://www.tandf.co.uk/journals for allowing me to republish some of the ethnographic material and analyses that appeared in B. A. West, Segments of Self and Other: The Magyar Hungarian Case, *National Identities*, 2000, 2(1):49–64.

I would like to thank the editors at the Women and International Development Program, Michigan State University. Some data and analyses in chapters 6 and 7 of this book previously appeared in Barbara A. West, Nation Under Siege, Bodies Under Siege: Security as a Gendered Category in Hungarian National Identity, May 1997, Working Papers on Women in International Development #260.

I would also like to thank *The Anthropology of East Europe Review*. Material from almost every chapter of this book first appeared in Barbara A. West, The Danger is Everywhere! Discourse on Security in Post-Socialist Hungary, 1994, 12(2):17–25.

I dedicate this book to my Grandma Walsh.

CHAPTER 1

Introduction

I sat in the dark, smoky, Hungarian café and watched as a group of burly men in tracksuits and leather jackets carried on their illicit exchange. Large rolls of money passed between them, a few words were exchanged, and then they were gone, leaving only the pungent smell of their Eastern European cigarettes behind. I didn't even have time to look away and pretend I wasn't watching their activity in the doorway before it was all over. The young woman behind the counter continued to dry glasses, the other two customers sipped their drinks and carried on with their private conversation. "Perfectly normal situation," I told myself, as I tried to formulate a sentence in Hungarian to ask for milk for my tea. However, before I could summon up the nerve to disturb the silence with my awkwardly phrased request, the phone behind the counter rang, startling me with its hollow, rattling tone. The woman drying glasses didn't answer. It rang a second time; she picked up another glass. Suddenly, one of the money men, as I thought of them, hurried back into the café, reached behind the counter, and answered the phone. Without saying a word, he hung up two or three seconds later, lit a cigarette, and helped himself to an aperitif of some sort.

By this time my I'd resolved myself to drinking my tea without milk, so I sipped along with him as we both waited for the next set of events to unfold. We didn't have long to wait. Before he'd even finished his drink he was joined by a group of five other men. This time, to avoid being caught watching their transactions I turned my chair slightly to look out the window. The view was misleading because the tinted glass made the sunny day appear dark and foreboding. I thought about the illegal money changing going on behind me and wondered if I was going to be roughed up on only my second day in Hungary. A few people walked past my window without turning their heads to see me watching them. I finished my tea and began to pull on my coat when a flurry of activity behind me made me turn and look. The men were all scrambling to leave the café, some out the front door, some down a dark hallway in the

1

back that led to the restrooms and a rear exit. I quickly turned away from their commotion to face the window and saw two uniformed police officers approach the café. They were clearly trying to see through the dark tinted glass. One of them even put his head right up to the window and shaded his eyes to get a better look, but by that time all he could have seen was a startled U.S.-American woman with her coat half on and a young Hungarian barmaid wiping out an ashtray. When they moved off a minute or two later the men who had gone into the back hallway immediately reappeared at the counter and picked up their drinks and cigarettes as if nothing had happened. I continued putting my coat on and just as I was leaving these men were joined by their two accomplices who'd left through the front door. As we passed each other in the doorway one of them gave me my first *kezét csokolom*, a fairly formal greeting for women that means, literally, I kiss your hand.

Many months later, when I told a Hungarian acquaintance about the first time I'd had my hand "kissed" in this way, she became angry that on my second day in Hungary I had been welcomed by such dangerous characters. "You see what it's like here," she said, "you can't even sit down for a drink in Szeged anymore without something happening." I can't say I ever felt the same anger over this kind of situation that my Hungarian acquaintances did, but I did eventually come to understand their perspective and where it came from.

This ethnography is about two different kinds of people trying to give voice to the experiences of the transition from socialism in Hungary. The most prominent and important people in the book are the Hungarian men and women who lived in Szeged, Hungary in the early to mid-1990s. These people were experiencing the worst unemployment and highest inflation rates their country had seen in decades. Perhaps more important, many also were grappling with the uncertainty of not knowing exactly what was going to happen as the single-party political system, with its command economy and restrictions on individual freedoms, dissolved itself and made way for new structures. Throughout the book I explore the ways many of these people participated in the construction of a new Hungarian society and identity through their local experiences and the language they used to talk about those experiences. For many, the lawlessness with which I began this introduction was representative of the most dominant forces at work in framing their new society and identities.

The other kind of person in this book is a young, female anthropologist from the United States who is not only trying to understand Hungary's political, economic, and social structures, but also the very process of how she is to reach that understanding. Throughout the book I talk about the process of participant observation, how my own biases and past experiences affected the experiences I had in the field, and how I came to understand Hungary and Hungarians throughout my seventeen months of fieldwork. My intention is not to compare my experiences with those of my informants, but to be as honest as possible about how I learned about their lives, what I felt during this process, and what sorts of cultural and personal baggage I carried with me during my time in Hungary. Of course, another anthropologist would have had a different experience and would be telling a somewhat different story. It is my hope, however, that I have provided enough ethnographic detail to allow readers to judge for themselves whether my analyses truly capture the essence of what these particular Hungarians were doing, saying, and feeling in the early to mid-1990s.

The primary question I hoped to answer during my research was, "What does it mean to be Hungarian in the early years of the collapse of socialist hegemony?" The simple response to this question is: To be a Hungarian in Szeged in 1993–94 was to be insecure. However, this simple answer requires explication on a number of fronts. First, the very identification of someone as "Hungarian" is not a simple, static, or self-evident process and must be explained in both its historical and cultural dimensions. I begin this explanation in this introduction, look at its historical dimensions in the following chapter, and continue to explore different facets of Hungarian identity throughout the book. Second, different kinds of Hungarians are experiencing the transition from socialism in different ways. For the purposes of this book, however, I have only focused on those differences created by geography and gender; I leave it to other anthropologists to explore race, class, and other differences. Third, the concept of insecurity can encompass everything from an individual body to an entire nation-state. Throughout the ethnographic chapters of this book I allow my Hungarian informants to explain in their own words what they meant when they talked about insecurity.

Context: Preceding Events

Since the summer of 1989 the countries of the former Soviet bloc have undergone tremendous change. One after the other the old Communist parties disappeared and new parties and coalitions appeared ready to lead their countries into the postsocialist era, so labeled because communism was never achieved but a form of socialism was. Of course, the change wasn't as easy as this sentence implies. For example, both hardline and reformed Communist parties jockeyed for positions in the new Polish and Hungarian governments and these parties won early elections in Bulgaria and Albania. Reformed socialist parties were elected in Hungary, Poland, and elsewhere after less than four years of transition. In Romania, the first "free" election brought a social order very much like that created by their last dictator, Ceausescu. Once underway, however, the transition from socialism created an atmosphere in which no category, concept, symbol, or reference point could be taken for granted. After forty years of communist ideology dominating all public space, every member of society became free to reevaluate and reconceptualize politics, economics, civil society, and social life, even to the degree of choosing socialist parties to lead their countries away from Soviet-style socialism.

In order to comprehend why in Hungary the concept of security loomed so large in many people's understanding of life in their home, city, and nation, it is important to understand the political, social, and economic situation Hungarians had come to know during the latter years of the socialist system. To begin with, Hungary under Kádár, the country's leader from 1956–88, was in no way the USSR under Stalin, Romania under Ceausescu, or East Germany under Honecker. Hungarians did not stand in bread lines or experience hunger, apart from a few months in 1956 and 1957 due to the failed revolution. Indeed, for the most part, life in Hungary during the latter decades of the socialist era was fairly comfortable. The paternalist socialist system provided employment, education, health care, housing, and permission to leave Hungary and even the other Warsaw Pact countries now and again. Szeged's proximity to the border with what was then Yugoslavia also allowed many people to purchase Western goods unavailable in other regions of Hungary or the other COMECON (Council for Mutual Economic Assistance) countries. Provided one was willing to work several jobs, keep silent, and play along with the lies promulgated by the socialist system, life in Hungary from the late 1960s through the late 1980s was fairly secure.

Indeed, security was the very idea used by the Kádár regime to legitimate his rule, at least from the late 1960s onward. In comparison with Ceausescu in socialist Romania, who used the concept of the nation to legitimate his tyrannical rule (Verdery 1991a), the Hungarian Socialist Workers' Party, with Kádár at its helm, was afraid to use the idea of the nation to legitimate the party or its government. The fear was that excessive nationalistic fervor would devolve into bloody conflict, as it had in 1956 when Moscow sent tanks and soldiers to Budapest to quell a revolution. Therefore, rather than national symbols and rhetoric as the primary source of legitimacy, Kádár relied on "paternalist concessions to the population," in the form of increased tolerance for consumerism, protection from arbitrary governmental harassment, freedom to enjoy the private sphere, and existential security (Fehér 1982:69, 71–2). The strategy was relatively successful in Hungary because it combined material comforts with an identity structure based on "the belief in being the 'most comfortable barrack in the [Soviet] camp'" (Markus 1982:91).

Therefore, despite their rejection of his system at the end of the 1980s, Kádár's long reign (November 1956–May 1988) remains a period of which many Hungarians are quite proud because he practiced a politics of reconciliation rather than adopting the confrontational style of his predecessors. His rule is perhaps best symbolized by his use of the phrase "All those who are not against us are with us" (cited in Berend 1990:386). Whereas his Stalinist predecessor, Rákosi, had demanded active participation in the building of a socialist state, Kádár required only acquiescence. In response to this leadership style, the people of Hungary generally traded their right to speak out against the government and party elite for "guarantees of existential security" (Kis 1989:235). As a result, most Hungarians spent these decades building their private lives and secondary sources of income. They also lived under the delusion that they were harder working and their government more competent than the citizens and governments of the other countries held in Moscow's sphere of influence by the Red Army, the Warsaw Pact, and COMECON (Kis 1989:236).

It is important to emphasize, however, that although Kádár himself had popular and legitimate support based on the security he provided, the political structure that provided his legitimacy (and their security) did not (Heller 1982:46). By the mid-1980s, the Hungarian state was no longer able to deliver on its end of the bargain and this support withered. Centralized planning, a huge foreign debt, and unfavorable economic relations within COMECON, including dependency on Soviet raw materials and energy sources, cut the real purchasing power of Hungarian citizens and brought the Hungarian mixed economy to a virtual standstill. In May 1988 the economic and political bankruptcy of party leadership under Kádár precipitated a change in state and party leadership, in which Kádár, along with eight of his Politburo members, were replaced by younger, more reform-minded party technocrats.

By 1989, these kinds of internal changes, combined with Gorbachev's renunciation of the Brezhnev doctrine, brought Hungary to an extraordinary "window of opportunity" (Szelenyi 1990:236). Politically, Hungary saw the rapid formation of alternative political parties, including the Magyar Democratic Forum (MDF), which led the first coalition government formed after free elections in 1990. Economically, the increased "petit bourgeoisification" of Hungary's economy allowed people to begin thinking about possible transformations for the entire economic structure (Szelenyi 1990). Finally, the collapse of Communist Parties throughout Eastern and Central Europe without a reaction from Moscow signaled to both Hungary's socialist leaders and the opposition that attempts at change would not result in another 1956.

Politically, Hungary seemed to change itself almost overnight. The round-table negotiations that began in the summer of 1989 transformed opposition groups into real political parties, which, unlike Solidarity in Poland, would not act without the mandate of a popular election. Despite their low membership numbers, the opposition groups MDF and SzDSz (Alliance of Free Democrats), who were later joined by FIDESZ (Young Democrats), a reconstituted Independent Smallholders' Party, and others completed "the transition from social movements to political parties . . . in months rather than years" (Bruszt and Stark 1991:242). As a result, even before the actual elections in the spring of 1990, party politics in Hungary dominated most public discourse and left the development of voluntary organizations and other aspects of civil society for later (Bruszt and Stark 1991:243). In March and April 1990 sixty-five percent of the Hungarian population went to the polls and elected an MDF-led coalition government; they were joined by the Independent Smallholders' Party and Christian Democrats while SzDSz and FIDESZ became the primary opposition parties. Hungary's "abrupt transition" from a single-party-dominated state to "entrenched parliamentarianism" (Bruszt and Stark 1991:243) was completed in ten months.

Economically, the MDF coalition pursued many different and contradictory goals, from the parceling out of collectivized land to small farmers and urban dwellers who had no equipment or capital to use or develop the land, to a tax system that favored foreign investors over Hungarians (Szelenyi 1992:233). Due to these inconsistencies, as well as corruption, misdirected priorities, and lack of commitment to economic issues, many Hungarians said that this party of historians and folklore specialists knew nothing about running a government. Like many others, I found that "a climate of dissatisfaction became all-pervasive" in Hungary not long after the elections in 1990 (Tismaneanu 1992:261).

The reasons given for the political, economic, and social changes that occurred in Eastern and Central Europe in 1989–1990 often address such systemic causes as economic failure, moral bankruptcy, and Gorbachev's reversal of the Brezhnev doctrine. Approaching the events from the actors' point of view, Mihaly Simai states, "people wanted greater transparency, predictability, stability, and the end of the era of constant worries deriving from an incalculable and unaccountable political power" (1992:55). The legitimacy of "state paternalism" that the Socialist Workers' Party and its government had enjoyed in Hungary evaporated when the state could no longer provide economic, political, or social security. Hungarians were ready in 1989 to remake their political and economic systems in pursuit of the kind of security no longer provided by state socialism. At the same time, their long-acknowledged identity as the "most comfortable barrack in the camp" (Markus 1982:91) had to be abandoned and new identities sought. Without knowing what the future would bring, both the new leadership and the Hungarian people turned to legitimating ideologies and concepts rooted in Hungary's past. The nation, border between East and West, and security are all ideas used in the early and mid-1990s in Hungary to talk about the process of rebuilding their personal, local, and national identities. This book focuses largely on the ways in which insecurity, one of the primary causes of discontent with the old socialist system, came to dominate much discourse on life in the early postsocialist era as well.

Szeged and Security

Szeged is located in the Hungarian Republic, a small central European country with an area of 35,919 square miles, or one percent of Europe (Bernstein 1990:7). Hungary shares borders with Slovakia and Ukraine to the north; Romania to the east; Serbia, Croatia, and Slovenia to the south; and Austria to the west. The population of this country today is 10.1 million people (it was slightly larger when I arrived in 1993), one fifth of whom live in Budapest, the capital, while eight other cities claim populations in excess of 100,000. Ethnically the country is comprised largely of Magyars, or ethnic Hungarians, although at least five percent are of Romany [Gypsy] descent and ethnic Germans, Romanians, Slovaks, and Southern Slavs can also be found throughout the country.

Szeged itself has a population of almost 200,000. It is characterized geographically by its location at the confluence of the Tisza and Maros rivers, as well as its position in the Alföld, or Great Plain, in the center of the Carpathian Basin, a large, flat, plains area surrounded by low mountain chains. The climate is typical of continental Europe; hot, dry summers and cold winters are separated by beautifully temperate springs and autumns. In addition, Szeged enjoys more hours of sunshine than anywhere else in central Europe, averaging more than two thousand hours per year and thus claiming the title of "The Sunshine City." In relation to its neighbors, Szeged is located fifteen kilometers from an official border crossing with Serbia and about the same distance from the Romanian boundary, although the closest legal border crossing is farther away. During my fieldwork, these features, in conjunction with the open border policies adopted by the Hungarian government at the time, were the most important factors in determining the face and character of the city, according to many of its residents.

The characteristics that first attract the attention of visitors to this county capital differ significantly depending on where the visitor is coming from. For example, the visitor from Budapest first notices the village-like atmosphere of the city and the traditional peasant architecture that dominates many residential neighborhoods. The many visitors who came to Szeged from Romania and the former Yugoslavia in the early 1990s first noticed the abundance and selection of consumer goods and foodstuffs available in every store and market. As a U.S.-American arriving in Szeged in January 1993, my attention

Author's first impression of Szeged.

was first captured by the crumbling facades of the once-beautiful nineteenth-century buildings that line the main pedestrian passageways of the city and most of its streets, roads, and boulevards. As time passed and I became more acquainted with Szeged and its residents, I became less cognizant of the crumbling facades and more aware of the ways these Hungarians believed their interior spaces—their own bodies, families, and nation—were crumbling more quickly than even their beautiful buildings. I was also pleasantly surprised in 1996 and again in 1999 when I revisited Szeged and found the city had undergone a facelift and many of these crumbling facades had been repaired or replaced.

Although I lived in Szeged for my entire time in Hungary, a part-time teaching job in Budapest and many trips to towns and cities all over Hungary afforded me the opportunity to think of Szeged in relation to other areas of the country. Indeed, it is only after leaving Szeged for a six day trip to western Hungary in May 1993 that I began to understand what a professor of history from Budapest, who also teaches part-time in Szeged, first said to me when he learned of my field site. "Szeged," he said to me in English, "is a special place in Hungary." When I asked him to explain, he said I should know even better than he does what this means because I am a U.S.-American. At the time I was baffled but could not get him to say more.

It was only after speaking with Hungarians who live in the capital and in the western border region and then returning again to Szeged that I realized what he might have meant. Hungarians often define themselves through opposition to the residents and characteristics of Serbia and Romania (West 2000). Due to their location near the borders of both nations, many Hungarians in Szeged have a heightened awareness of their Hungarianness, their marginality within Hungary, their proximity to these borders, and their local Szeged identity. In contrast, Hungarians who live in cities on the Austrian and Slovak borders did not make immediate reference to marginality, borders, or the large number of foreigners who cross them daily when I asked about their experiences of the transition from socialism, as happened frequently in Szeged. I was never able to get my acquaintance to clarify what he meant by his statement that Szeged is a special place. Nevertheless, I have found many things that have allowed me to repeat it, not the least of which is the specifically Szeged experience of postsocialist life that produced a distinct local feeling of insecurity. With regard to his statement that as a U.S.-American I should understand Szeged's specialness even more than Hungarians, I can only guess that he was referring to the outsiders' ability to see things that are invisible to an insider.

I found in the marginalized border city of Szeged that while Western observers of the transition spoke in the early to mid-1990s of privatization and global markets, the people of Szeged spoke of economic insecurity, including unemployment and inflation. While the Hungarian government spoke largely of open borders and joining Europe, the people I met spoke of national, local, and personal insecurity and their fears of crime; the influx of non-Magyar languages, identities, and customs; and foreigners themselves. The one thing shared by most of my acquaintances in Szeged during my first year and a half in Hungary, women and men, pensioners and students, factory workers and intellectuals, was a concern with security. Indeed, Hungarians in Szeged in 1993–94 tended to define all social processes and relationships in terms of security. Their social idiom was a security idiom.

Once I began to understand the paternalism of the socialist system and compare it to what I knew of capitalism, their concern with security seemed entirely rational and even appropriate. Unemployment was high at 10.4% (www.ems.psu.edu), inflation was even higher at 22.5% (users.ox.ac.uk), and the elimination of the paternal authority of the Kádár system had left Hungary with an economy in which individual initiative, luck, and connections provided the only access to security. There was no guaranteed employment or living wage system and people were afraid for their future, as well as that of their children and parents. At the same time, the words and actions that kept coming into focus as I began to understand Hungarians' concern with security did not solely pertain to the economic sphere. The security of the Hungarian nation, by which I mean the social construction of the Hungarian people rather than the political construction of the Hungarian state, was also a great concern for many people in Szeged at that time. Almost any discussion, whether it was concerned with holidays, families, friends, shopping, or housing got tied up into a discourse on the dangers for the Hungarian nation and of being Hungarian, especially a Hungarian woman. To be Hungarian in the postsocialist era, according to those living in the marginalized southern borderland, was to be insecure.

This insecurity seems on the surface to coincide with the concerns of both indigenous political leaders in eastern and central Europe and of many academics from both inside and outside this region since 1990. However, the concern of Hungary's central government was with a phenomenon that Vojtech Mastny calls a "security limbo" (in Michta 1992:xiii) or what Stephen Larrabee (1992) calls "a security vacuum in Eastern Europe" (Larrabee 1993:xii). All of these authors are writing of the "uncertain and unstable security environment" caused in part by "the disintegration of the former USSR; the crisis in Yugoslavia; the breakup of Czechoslovakia" (Larrabee 1993:xi). They refer primarily to international borders, military strengths and alliances, and state sovereignty. Like the Hungarian security statement passed by the Parliament on March 2, 1993, much of the work on Hungarian and central European security generally emphasizes military strength and defense against international aggression. Security for them is calculated in terms of defense budgets, artillery and air strike capacity, troop numbers, foreign treaties, and the like.

The problem with these formulations in light of my research is that they refer only to the security of the state. What I found, however, is the Hungarian state is one of the few areas in which the people of Szeged feel relatively secure. The people I know in Hungary were more worried about the security of Hungarian national culture and language and with the security of their own bodies, jobs, and futures than they were with the collapse of either the former Soviet Union or the former Czechoslovakia. My observations in this one provincial city are similar to the views published in an article in the national newspaper *Népszabadság* citing Hungarian public opinion polls done in both 1990 and 1992; the article states that "national defense" was rated last in a list of problems affecting postsocialist Hungary in both years in which the poll was conducted (4/7/92:1, 6). Even Yugoslavia as it existed in 1991, the government of which described Hungary as "the main front of Western activities" against them (Gagnon 1991:26), concerned Hungarians in Szeged more in cultural and economic terms than in terms of military invasion. An analysis of the situation in Hungary in the mid-1990s, as it was constructed and experienced by members of the Szeged community, must acknowledge "security involves more than just military threats and structures" (Jackson 1992:15).

The concept that best describes the concerns of the Hungarians I spoke and lived with in the early and mid-1990s is "societal security" (Wæver 1993). Societal security expresses a

> concern . . . with the ability of a society to persist in its essential character under changing conditions and possible or actual threats. More specifically, it is about the sustainability, within acceptable conditions for evolution, of traditional patterns of language, culture, association, and religious and national identity and custom. . . . Societal security is about situations when societies perceive a threat in identity terms. (Wæver 1993:23)

Many members of the Szeged community in the early and mid-1990s were relatively unconcerned with military treaties and mobilization preparedness; the Hungarian state was seen as relatively secure on both a global and regional scale. People in Szeged were generally unperturbed by the NATO rejection of their government's desire for immediate entry in 1994. Prime Minister József Antall's death in December 1993 did not move Hungarians to question their country's safety at the hands of foreign military or political powers. Even the frequent violations of Hungarian airspace over Szeged by Yugoslavian military jets in 1993–94 were accepted as part of daily life on the border.

On the other hand, Hungarians in Szeged spoke of invasions of foreign shoppers, of border infractions by entrepreneurs and consumers as if these tourists and businesspeople were foreign soldiers sent to Szeged to wipe out this outpost of Hungarian culture, along with its Magyar inhabitants. Because of the proximity of two international boundaries, daily life in Szeged and the borderland in which it is located was experienced as out of control and spoken of in terms more appropriate, perhaps, for southeast Hungary in 1920, when Serbian, Romanian, and French soldiers did occupy the region. Unemployment, crime, inflation, corruption, and other societal security concerns were likewise seen as threatening to the nation and its members as Hungarians. They feared the economic might of foreign shoppers and saw accommodations to them, such as signs and advertisements in Serbo-Croatian, as threatening to Hungarian culture. In short, they were concerned for their nation as a "collective individual," their societal security, and as a "collection of individuals" (Handler 1988), their personal security as members of the Hungarian nation.

Research in the City of Sunshine

My focus on the concepts of security and nation in Hungary is based on seventeen months of participant observation research in Szeged. I have also revisited Szeged during the summers of 1996 and 1999 to do other research, but these trips provided only peripheral information for this work. I chose to do my doctoral research in central Europe after watching the Communist Party regimes in that region collapse in 1989 and 1990. I chose Hungary specifically because of a wonderful spring break I had spent there in 1988 and because few outsiders were interested in learning their very difficult, non-European language.

During my months in Szeged, I kept foremost in my thoughts the idea that everything I was to see, hear, and experience could provide cultural knowledge and insight into the ways Hungarians imagine themselves in the world. For fifteen months between January 1993 and March 1994, followed by two additional months during the summer of 1994, I lived in this Hungarian border city with another anthropologist, who was engaged in her own research project. Throughout this time in Hungary I tried to make friends; collected life histories and time-use surveys; read newspapers; listened to radio; attended cultural, political, and social events; and, like most Hungarians, worked several unofficial jobs. In addition, I supplemented information taken from these sources by holding single-issue interviews with dozens of people that lasted anywhere from half an hour to three hours with any one person. These interviews were constructed around such topics as family; relatives; friends; holidays; mutual aid, especially during times of emergency; marriage; divorce; death; politics; education; work; and the ways all these may have been different in the past. During the first few months of my fieldwork I sought out people who could speak some English, so we could exchange conversation each in our own native language. After about six months in Hungary my language skills had improved, with the help of two fantastic tutors, to the degree that most people were more comfortable speaking with me in Hungarian. Most of my interviews, life histories, and data were gathered in Hungarian and translated by me, with Michelle Landers's help (see West 1997).

The end result of this reliance on such a wide array of sources is a book that embraces and includes the voices, opinions, and experiences of many members of the Hungarian community in Szeged. In case studies of garden owners and non-owners, as well as people's descriptions of their holidays, friendships, and families, I look to the mundane experiences of postsocialist life to tell us something important about the ways Hungarians in Szeged imagined themselves and their nation at that time. In addition to the ordinary, I also look to the extraordinary, events such as elections, bus trips, and murders. In every case I allow my acquaintances from Szeged to speak. At the same time, I place the information and interpretations from my interviews, conversations, and participant observation side by side with information from local and national newspapers and political campaign material. In other words, rather than avoiding diversity and polyphony, I have embraced them and used them to present as complete a picture as possible of Hungarians' experiences in the transition from socialism.

Throughout this book I address the ways security discourse was used by people in Szeged to define themselves, their community, and their nation in a postsocialist context. In the next chapter I look at Hungarian history and the way the Hungarian national community in the mid-1990s was imagined to flow naturally from this history. I find it is impossible to understand the postsocialist situation in Hungary without looking back to what came before. However, because I was not in Hungary as anything but a tourist prior to the end of the socialist era, this chapter depends on the research of others.

The ethnographic body of the book, based on my own fieldwork, explores some of the most salient experiences of postsocialist Hungarian life in Szeged and shows the ways these experiences are used by people in this community to construct a coherent set of identities for themselves and the nation. In one chapter I explore kinship and other relationships, and holidays and other rituals as they were experienced in Szeged in 1993–94. I then make the argument, following Cohen (1996), that the values, norms, and experiences of members of these networks—local communities that share a set of experiences within a common temporal and spatial framework—provide some of the constructs with which the more abstract national community is imagined. The insecurities commonly believed to be plaguing the nation as a whole are shown to have their parallels in the ways these Hungarians are experiencing the transition in their personal lives. In the next chapter I look at the ways that the use of agriculture to characterize Hungarians in the last two centuries was reinvented and transformed in the early years of the transition. Through the use of case studies of gardeners and non-gardeners I make the argument that, in part, to be Hungarian is to work the land. In a third ethnographic chapter I explore the ways many Hungarians imagine themselves in relation to others, including their "Balkán" neighbors and "Europe," by relating my experiences with some U.S.-American and Hungarian friends on a shopping bus traveling through the former Yugoslavia and Bulgaria to Istanbul, Turkey and a subsequent bus trip to France. In chapter 6, I explore a transformation I witnessed in the use of insecurity as the defining feature of the postsocialist Hungarian nation. Following a much-discussed murder in Szeged, politicians and the local media began to participate in the construction of an identity for Hungary based on the idea of insecurity, as my informants had been doing for the previous year. Finally, I conclude the ethnographic part of the book with an examination of the construction of national identities as a series of gendered processes. I go back to the ethnographic data presented in the previous chapters and show some of the ways gendered representations of the nation and its members and gender-specific experiences of these members are used to naturalize certain views of the nation. I conclude with a chapter that summarizes the arguments made throughout the book, and an Epilogue, which presents a short discussion of an eight-week trip back to Szeged in the summer of 1996, two full years after the original research project. This trip reinforced for me the strength of the arguments I make in this book concerning the use of insecurity in the imagining of the Hungarian nation. If anything, 1996 found my acquaintances feeling even more insecure in the world than they had in 1994.

Arrival

I conclude this introduction with a narrative describing my entrée to the world of the fieldworker. It has been an interesting experience for me to relive this time in my life through the process of reading my journals and writing this narrative. I have found many of the Hungarian experiences and feelings that became so familiar to me after seventeen months in the field were evident from the very beginning, if only I hadn't been so caught up in my own fear and excitement to take notice of them.

My first impressions of the Szeged area came to me from the back of a taxi as I was driven south from Budapest to Szeged. I hadn't meant to allow the unofficial driver who picked me up at the train station in Budapest to drive me the three hours to my fieldwork site, but at the time it just seemed easier to pay him for this service than to fight with him about it; lug my two giant duffel bags, backpack, and laptop computer around Budapest; pay for a hotel that night; and get on a train the following day. Despite being overcharged, I still believe I made the right decision. I arrived in Szeged a day ahead of schedule, spoke my first words of Hungarian with someone who spoke no English, and even understood a little bit of what he said to me.

I also appreciate the opportunity the ride gave me to see the landscape in that area of Hungary. The aspect I most highlighted in my journal later that week was the apparent emptiness of the region, which was interrupted only occasionally by small, mostly abandoned-looking farms surrounded by old trees and dilapidated fences. This was clearly very different from the hilly, agricultural area I had seen in western Hungary when I vacationed there in 1988 and that had greeted me hours earlier when I entered Hungary by train from Austria. This view would have provided my first hint at the importance of land and farming to Hungarians, and the problem of unused fields at the end of the socialist era, if only I knew what to look for. At that time, however, I was unaware of the meaning of almost everything I saw and heard so all I could do was observe carefully and hope for the best.

The same was also true as I approached Szeged, when tall, uniform apartment blocks appeared in an arc curving around the outskirts of the city, much as they had done outside of the two large towns through which I had passed on my long drive from the capital. In 1988 I had stayed in a neighborhood such as this in Budapest, but I did not expect to see such stark uniformity outside of the capital. I hoped the inner areas of Szeged, like these other town centers through which I had passed, contained more interesting and attractive architecture. When I did finally get into the center of Szeged, I was not disappointed.

However, I did not have the opportunity to enter Szeged that first evening to discover whether I had agreed to live in a city of nothing but uniform cement buildings because my driver adamantly refused to enter the city. He pulled off the road at the first truck drivers' motel we spotted along the road, dropped me off at the curb, took his money, and then quickly locked his doors and sped away. At the time I figured he was just unfamiliar with Szeged and anxious to get back to Budapest. It wasn't until after I had been in the field for over a year that I realized his concern was probably not so much the result of his unfamiliarity with Szeged, but of the many stories he would have heard about it as a dangerous border city. In my state of blissful ignorance at the time, it never occurred to me this relatively small (by U.S.-American standards) county capital would be at all frightening to this man who, to me, seemed to have all the nerve in the world.

That first night in the motel I was so tired it wouldn't have mattered where the driver had dropped me off. I settled into my room and went downstairs to find the restaurant. It was a pleasant enough place, with enough women customers to make me feel comfortable in a room filled with male truck drivers. I was much too tired to linger over the meal for long anyway and went upstairs almost immediately. After a quick bath I fell into the narrow twin bed, which was covered with a tiny sheet that did not tuck into anything or even fully cover the upholstered mattress. I shocked myself that night by sleeping for more than eleven hours. I found during my first few weeks in Hungary the need for excessive amounts of sleep was just one of many physical manifestations of the exhaustion and stress caused by my entry into this unfamiliar country with its, for me, difficult language and bewildering customs.

On that first morning, however, I woke up relatively refreshed, despite the fact that the small sheet I had been given to sleep on was balled up at my feet and my face was imprinted with the pattern of the woolly, textured upholstery of the bed. I was able to laugh at the condition of my face that morning, since I did not realize I would wake up that way every day for a year and a half. Unfortunately, all of the sheets I used during my time in Szeged were significantly smaller than the beds they were meant to cover and they always wound up in a ball, either at my feet or my head.

Nonetheless, on that first morning, I awoke ready to begin the adventure of exploring Szeged, trying to find the one person whose name I had been given by a mutual acquaintance in the United States, and getting a cheaper place to stay until I found more permanent accommodations. First on the agenda, however, I needed breakfast. I went back down to the motel's dining room, only to find all the women with whom I had shared the room with the truck drivers were absent. Odd, I thought, but then put it out of my mind as the waitress delivered the hot, exceptionally sweet fruit drink the menu called tea, along with rolls and scrambled eggs with cheese. It didn't occur to me until dinner that evening, when the women reappeared in the dining room, why they had been absent from breakfast. After dinner I lingered over a pot of English tea, which I discovered meant tea as I knew it instead of the sweet beverage from breakfast, and watched as one at a time the women entered, drank a cup of coffee, went out to the parking lot, and then came back twenty to thirty minutes later to repeat the process. It suddenly dawned on me what was going on; these women were prostitutes. The next day I confirmed with my language tutor that I was, indeed, staying in Szeged's largest house of prostitution.

However, that morning, still ignorant of the criminal activity taking place at my motel and of the potential danger my tutor cited, I finished breakfast and set out to begin my exploration of Szeged. I was greeted at the edge of the city by a bewildering sight: large pipes, probably two feet in diameter, ran along the ground in some places, hung suspended from buildings and bridges in others, and connected a series of buildings. This was clearly some sort of factory compound but what they manufactured and the reason for the external pipes was a mystery. I later learned this was Szeged's textile factory and the pipes, which can be seen all over Hungary, carry steam from a central generating plant to the buildings or areas where it is needed. On this first walk into town I also noticed the crumbling stucco, exposed brick, and other signs that pollution and poverty were taking their toll on many of Szeged's buildings.

As I walked, I found myself feeling increasingly concerned that I had decided to live in such a grimy and deteriorating industrial area. Fortunately, this feeling could not last long. I soon entered Szeged's main square, Széchenyi Square, and saw the beautiful, yellow, Eclectic-Baroque style building of the city hall, the fountains and carefully tended flower beds that would come to life in the spring, and the acres of grass divided in two by a wide pedestrian path that leads out of the park area to become the main pedestrian shopping district in the center of the city. At the other end of this pedestrian route I found the main gathering place for Szeged, Dugonics Square, which is surrounded by the József Attila University library at one end, the Burger King and a large department store at one corner, a large street on the other end, and smaller streets lined with shops on the two sides. A year later one particular shop on this square would also become the primary symbol of the dangers felt by all Hungarians in Szeged, but, like everyone else at the time, I was ignorant of its importance in those terms.

The primary attraction of this square for most of my time in Hungary was not this shop but the fountain in the center. The concrete benches surrounding this fountain were almost always covered with mothers watching their small children, nursery school teachers who brought their classes to play at the fountain, young couples holding hands or kissing, university students enjoying a break from work in the library, and older people resting from their walk through town or merely enjoying watching the activity in the heart of the city. Since I had arrived in Szeged in the midst of an unseasonably warm spell and was enjoying temperatures hovering around ten degrees Celsius (around fifty Fahrenheit) I enjoyed watching all of this activity at the fountain as I took advantage of the benches to sit and formulate a plan for locating my contact at the university, a man named Tibor, whom, I had been told, did not have a telephone at home.

The task didn't turn out to be as difficult as I had imagined. I waylaid a young woman on her way into the university library to ask for directions to my contact's office. After an earnest attempt to make me understand her directions, she kindly walked me to the humanities building and Tibor's office. At the time I was merely grateful to her for her kindness. It wasn't until later I realized how lucky I was to have found someone willing not only to speak with a stranger on the street, but to provide help. In the many months I have spent in Hungary subsequent to that first day, I have never again found a stranger on the street willing to carry on a conversation with me. I wonder if she was put at ease by my having made her laugh with my use of the formal pronoun and verb ending with her; I noted she used the informal ending with me. Hungarian, like many languages, uses several different words for "you." Not only are there different words for you-singular and you-plural, but there are also three different degrees of formality and respect that need to be expressed both with pronouns and verb endings. I eventually became familiar with these different terms and endings, although I am still not entirely comfortable with them, but on that first day it was all a mystery and I felt it was safer to be formal than to insult a total stranger. Apparently, I was being overly cautious.

When we finally arrived at my tutor's office, to my surprise and relief, I found my contact's home phone number tacked to the door. His wife, I knew from our mutual acquaintance, also spoke some English, so even if Tibor didn't answer the phone himself I could probably make do with some combination of English and Hungarian. I also hoped she would understand my unfamiliarity with the different versions of "you" and not laugh too hard at me. However, even if she did, I was feeling extremely good about myself. I had found my contact and received my first grammar lesson; clearly, I was on my way to being a fieldworker.

I spent the rest of my first week in Hungary trying to locate a room to rent from a family who was willing to speak Hungarian with me, learning new vocabulary words, and exploring the city. At that time I also began to feel better about my choice of fieldsite as I realized how laughable my first impression of Szeged as an industrial city had been. Because of its proximity to a less than friendly border with Yugoslavia, which, despite its Communist government, was neither a member of the Warsaw Pact nor its economic equivalent, Szeged never experienced the industrialization that characterized many other towns and cities in Soviet-dominated eastern and central Europe. In part because of this absence of an industrial base and in part because of the increasing centrality of Budapest, Szeged and its area has been defined by one of Hungary's leading political geographers as a marginal region (Tóth 1988), known more for its paprika and universities than any political or economic importance for the country as a whole. As I would learn later, Szeged is also known for its crime and danger, but in that first week I didn't understand any of the indicators of this fact.

Another factor that improved my attitude toward Szeged in those first few days is that after the second night I moved from the prostitute motel. I was not so much concerned about the dangers, as perhaps I should have been, but rather the cost and impersonal service of the motel did not make me feel like an anthropologist. I arranged for a room through a local tourist office and spent the rest of the week trying to communicate with the amiable older woman in whose apartment I found myself. In that situation it was much easier to feel like an anthropologist; she spoke with me often, praised my limited language skills, and invited me to come back and visit. In fact, six months later, after my language skills had greatly improved, I did go back and visit and even conducted interviews with this woman over a period of several months. However, at the outset, I only had the room for one week so I spent much of that time searching newspapers and bulletin boards for apartments and rooms for rent.

Exactly one week after my arrival in Szeged, I moved into my first permanent home. Tibor was a tremendous help during this first week, helping me find my home by telephoning the leads I found and speaking with the landladies. According to him, I was moving in with a retired schoolteacher

In the neighborhood of the author's first permanent home.

who wanted interesting students with whom to speak. I wasn't sure my limited vocabulary allowed me to be interesting in Hungarian, but I felt positive this was the perfect place for me: a private home in a village-like neighborhood about four kilometers from the city center, with a single, lonely woman who was willing not only to speak with me but help me to learn the language. There were drawbacks, of course, like the lack of a refrigerator and washing machine (in a city with no laundromats), but she did have a telephone, a pantry that not only kept food cold but occasionally froze my milk during winter cold spells, and easy access to what at the time was the best grocery store in the Szeged area. I moved in with Veronika during the first snowstorm of the season and, despite this bad omen, knew immediately I had chosen the perfect place to begin my career as a fieldworker.

That first night my patient landlady sat with me at my table and allowed me to show her my family photographs. The following afternoon she baked delicious pastries for me. In the evenings she told me about her work, patiently explaining terms to me that did not appear in my dictionary, and encouraged me to tell her about my language lessons or whatever else had engaged me during the day. Even after I moved from Veronika's house to a place closer to the city center, I continued to visit her and her daughter's family regularly throughout my time in Szeged. In 1996 and then again in 1999, when I returned for the summers, she welcomed me back with hugs and kisses and assured me I would always have a place to which I could return in Szeged.

CHAPTER 2

The Idea of the Hungarian Nation over Time

I have chosen to focus specifically on the category of the nation in Hungary because of the important role the national idea has played both during the transition from socialism throughout eastern and central Europe and in Hungarian history and historiography for more than a century and a half. Rather than the concept of statehood, which includes all citizens regardless of their ethnic or national background, and thus in Hungary includes Germans, Slovaks, other Slavs, Jews, and Roma (or Gypsies, as they are often called), the nation in Hungary has, since the mid-nineteenth century, been a community of ethnic Magyars. The members of this nation believe some of the traits that set them apart from these other Hungarian citizens are a common language, history, territory, religion, and value system constructed around agricultural work. From the mid-nineteenth century until the end of World War II, the idea of the Magyar nation in Hungary was used by many political parties and movements to justify their programs and limit the rights of other peoples living in the state. During the socialist years, especially following the revolution of 1956, the nation became a taboo subject in Hungary and the party elite replaced it with citizenship and socialist internationalism as ideas to rally Hungarians' loyalties and stir their feelings. Finally, when the socialist political structure was stripped away in 1988–90, the first concept used by opposition groups to declare their moral fitness to rule, their anticommunism, was that most eschewed by the socialist party leadership: the Hungarian nation.

In addition to being a useful tool for politicians to use to justify their ideas within Hungary, the Magyar nation has also been an important identity structure for ordinary Magyars, both inside and outside of Hungary. The concept of the nation allied Magyar peasants with the largely Magyar nobility against peasants of other nationalities living in Hungarian territory in the second half of the nineteenth century (Sugar 1969). The nation has been a major topic of study for Hungarian historians and ethnographers for over a century. The Magyar Hungarians I meet both in Hungary and elsewhere continue to speak with pride about their national community, the accomplishments of its famous members, and their difficult history as a unique linguistic and cultural community in central Europe. Clearly, as an anthropologist who wanted to study something of the utmost importance to my Hungarian informants, I had to focus my energy on the Magyar national community.

Studying the Nation

I begin with a definition of the concept of a nation generally, including a discussion of the ways I, as an anthropologist working in central Europe, may differ in my use of the term from those coming to it from other disciplines and other geographic regions. I consider nations to be constantly shifting communities of people who feel connected to one another based on *what they believe* is a common culture, history, territory, conception of the future, and political aspirations for a state. There is an element of "taken-for-grantedness" (Foster 1991:237) about national communities, as there is with band and tribal communities; they also are experienced as natural and timeless, as primordial. Yet, at the same time, since the members of nations do not know each other personally or interact with each other on a regular basis, nations have no reality outside of the processes through which their members come to believe in them. These processes involve different communities in the nation competing to have their "consciousness or perception of what the nation is or should be" become the accepted reality (Fox 1990:4). Nations have been called "imagined communities" (Anderson 1983) because they exist first and foremost in this consciousness or perception.

Having decided to focus my fieldwork project on studying the nation in Hungary, I next needed to develop some research method that would be appropriate both for an anthropologist and for understanding the worldview of such a large community. The primary problem for an anthropologist interested in this topic is the methods we employ to gain information were developed for use in small-scale societies and villages. Most everything I had read about doing fieldwork indicated I was supposed to know a majority of the people in the community I was studying, become intimately involved in their lives, and be invited to share their most personal and sacred events. Obviously, when my "community" was members of the Magyar nation who also lived in the Hungarian state, a group of nearly ten million people, I was not going to be able to meet even a tiny proportion of them, much less become intimately involved in their lives.

Fortunately, I was not the first anthropologist interested in studying a national community instead of a village community so I did have some examples to follow. The most important aspect of national communities for many anthropologists is that while appearing to be natural and timeless, they are, in fact, continuously being produced, reproduced, and challenged in the minds of both members and nonmembers. Some tools available to communities to produce and reproduce national identities in their members are national poetry, song, art, festivals and holidays, national stories or origin myths, and even the enactment of official state policy, if the members of the nation have been able to establish a state of their own, as Hungarians have. Therefore, in order to study national communities, some anthropologists have looked primarily at national poetry, festival, myth, and state policy, and done fieldwork with the producers of these materials.

I have two problems with this method, despite its many strengths when studying national communities. My first problem is a methodological one. I argue that studying nations through documents, festivals, and their producers does not allow anthropologists to do what they do best: tell their audience about the experiences of ordinary people living in a particular community. So, while I do look at a few examples of high culture throughout this book, I do so primarily to understand the way my Hungarian informants experienced them in their own lives. My second problem with this method concerns the assumptions about nations implicit in it. By studying nations through national myths, festivals, stories, and state policies, most of the people who consider themselves to be members of these nations are assumed to be culture consumers rather than producers. This approach assumes ordinary people's participation in the production of national culture is limited to their reading of national literature, retelling of national stories, or attendance at national festivals. In other words, they are seen as listeners rather than as active participants in the communicative system of the nation (Csepeli 1989:11–14). In reaction to this kind of assumption, I propose that ordinary members of nations also participate in the production of national cultures and identities to some degree. They are not blank slates upon which elite cultural and political actors can project their image of the nation. Rather, they are agents in this cultural production who reject some national images, stories, and characteristics because they are irrelevant or contradictory to their experiences, and who create other images, stories, and characteristics more in line with their own experiences.

In order to get around these difficulties and problematic assumptions, I propose, following Cohen (1996), that doing fieldwork with the members of a local community can provide some understanding of these members' experience of membership in the national community. Throughout this book, I explore the ways in which residence in the border city of Szeged in the mid-1990s, a community defined in terms of both space and time, circumscribed these Hungarians' abilities to imagine the nation as a whole. This is not to say that national identity is merely local identity on a larger scale. Rather, I posit that nations are imagined by members of local communities in and through their localized experiences and identities. I argue that members of the Szeged community imagine the nation as a whole through their experiences of living in their marginalized border city. These experiences do not provide the only categories through which the nation is imagined; however, I focus on them here because this method allows me both to explore the idea of nationhood and to draw on anthropology's greatest strengths.

In addition to the role of geography in helping individuals imagine the national community, I also am interested in the ways membership in communities defined by gender influence people's imagining of the nation and themselves as members. I argue that national communities become meaningful and powerful—they become part of an individual's reference for defining him- or herself—when they have been incorporated into individual bodies. The way individuals incorporate the idea of the nation into their own bodies is by engaging in activities defined as appropriate for members of that national community, not just political rituals and other solitary events that remind subjects of their national or local identities (Kürti 1990), but the daily practice of trafficking in the significant symbols (Geertz 1973:45) of the national community. As I discuss throughout this book, in Szeged in the early- to mid-1990s, this meant participating in private gardening, protecting oneself and one's family from random crime, and closing one's personal networks off from distant acquaintances, colleagues, and relatives.

While participation in these practices defines what it means to be a member of the Hungarian nation for many in Szeged, in my analysis I must pay attention to the fact that not everybody can participate in them in the same way. Men and women, old and young, worker and intellectual, urban and rural dwellers all experience these practices in very different ways. In general, how one experiences membership in a national community is contingent upon a large number of these different factors. At the end of this book I pay attention to the ways gender plays a very important role in the experience of membership in the national community. I argue that the cultural construction of nationhood, a publicly enacted system of symbols uniting a community of members, empowers and constrains women and men very differently and differentially affects their sense of belonging, the ways they imagine the nation itself, and their participation in it. To study this, I examine not only the experiences of men and women as members of the nation, but also the ways representations of the nation and of its members are likewise gendered in significant ways.

The Magyar Nation in Historical Perspective

The concept of the nation, as opposed to ethnic group or state, serves as a primary category of inclusion and exclusion in Hungary. The development of nationalism in central Europe dates to the period of the French Revolution (Anderson 1983), particularly the reign of Joseph II (1780–90) and his attempts at forcing Hungarians and other linguistic groups within the Habsburg empire to speak and read only German. At this time, many of these linguistic groups first began to recognize themselves as discrete political and cultural units, or nationalities. In Hungary, as everyplace else, different groups confronted the project of producing national culture with different notions of the (arbitrary) boundaries marking inclusion in and exclusion from this community.

Nobles, some of whom were not ethnically Magyar, often focused their energies on promoting a common language and political culture as the defining features of the "natio Hungarica" (Jászi 1961:27). Habsburg rulers attempted to limit their national language to the private sphere and to challenge the assumption that the Hungarian language was unsuitable for dealing with affairs of state. To counter this, Count István Széchenyi led a movement in the first decades of the nineteenth century for the development of national literature and education (Cushing 1960:461). Even today, the Hungarian language continues to be an important marker of belonging in the Magyar nation. Hungarians continue to talk about being alone in Europe because they are surrounded by neighbors who speak Germanic, Romance, or Slavic languages, which have no relation at all to their own. Magyar is a non-European language belonging to the Finno-Ugric language family, which means its only relationship to other languages spoken in Europe is a remote, structural similarity to Finnish and Estonian. Indeed, learning to speak and, to a lesser degree, read Hungarian was a constant reminder to me of this language's unique place in the world! The only Hungarian words recognizable to native English speakers are "paprika" and "gulyás," which, while important parts of Hungarian culture, only get one so far in day-to-day conversation.

Other communities within Hungary interested in constructing a unique national identity in the nineteenth century employed a discourse on religion, either in addition to or instead of language, in their efforts to naturalize their view of what it means to be Hungarian (György 1966:14). For example, some saw Hungary as a Christian buffer protecting Europe from the Muslim Turks (Glatz 1983). Others viewed Hungary as a Catholic nation protecting western Europe from Orthodoxy (Laszlo 1983). In a third construction of religious nationalism, some Magyar nobles converted to Calvinism or other Protestant denominations as a way to distinguish the Hungarian nation from Catholic Austria (Laszlo 1983).

During my time in Hungary, religion was a much less important marker of Hungarian nationality than it had been a century and a half earlier. I spoke with Hungarian Catholics, Jews, Methodists, Baptists, Baha'is, Hari Krishnas, Mormons, Pentecostals, Nazarenes, and "members of an Eastern religion," which seemed to be vaguely Buddhist, about their religious beliefs, practices, and affiliations, and not one of them made any connection between religion and membership in the nation. Of course, it is not unexpected that in a traditionally Catholic country members of other religions would not associate their religious beliefs and practices with the nation as a whole, but even Hungarian Catholics failed to make any connection between the national community and their religious community. Whether this was due to forty years of state-sanctioned atheism or some other factor, in the early- to mid-1990s I did not find religion to be a primary marker of inclusion in the Magyar national community.

In addition to language and religion, many nineteenth-century Hungarian nationalists were also influenced by Romanticism to look both to the peasantry and to the "lone cowboy" for what they saw as authentic national symbols in their quest to create a homogeneous national culture (Hofer 1991:146–47). Artifacts and customs from Hungary's so-called peasant and pastoral cultures that had been "invented" and transformed into national symbols by the nobility were adopted by all sectors of Magyar society (see Kisbán 1989). As Martha Lampland argues, "following the defeat of the War of Independence [in 1849] . . . [p]easants were heralded as the [*sic*] 'the fundamental element of the state' and agriculture was to be accorded sacred status within the economy" (1994:300). The aristocracy and other reformers did not use peasant folklore alone to legitimate the nation, but "the practice of agriculture" was also "elevated to the highest purpose: building the nation" (Lampland 1994:301).

A concern with peasants and pastoralists, as well as their lifeways and work, as markers of belonging in the Hungarian nation remained important throughout the twentieth century as well. In the interwar period, for example, Hungarian populist writers "sought a spiritual renewal that would redefine the relation between politics, art, and the peasantry through an indigenous 'Third Road' between communism and capitalism" (Gal 1991:446). These authors located "authentic Hungarian traditional values of community and work" in peasant culture and "they argued that the peasantry formed the true core of the nation" (Gal 1991:446). In the early 1990s, displays in the Ethnography and National Museums in Budapest, the Móra Ferenc Museum in Szeged, the county museum in Békéscsaba, and many others all gave a significant percentage of their display space to the art, work, and lifeways of the nineteenth-century Hungarian peasantry and pastoralists from earlier historical periods. Horse shows on the Hortobágy plain and other historical reenactments of this sort likewise draw upon the idea that, "for centuries the Hungarians have been known as a nation of riders" (Koppány 1999:27), although I did not find Hungarians for whom this image had contemporary significance. However, as I present throughout this book, supposed peasant values of work and agricultural production did continue to inform the construction of the national community in Hungary after the socialist era.

One result of this mix of ideas, and the policies enacted by Hungarian leaders to turn them into reality, was the birth of "Magyar nationalism and its political aspirations for a nation state" out of a "previously unpolitical national consciousness" in the nineteenth century (Hoensch 1988:4). A second result was the forced Magyarization of the non-Magyar majority living on Hungarian territory (Glatz 1983:43). In 1842, 5.57 million ethnic Magyars lived amongst 8.6 million Romanians, Slovaks, Germans, Croats, Serbs, Ukrainians, Slovenes, Jews, Roma, and others (Hoensch 1988:4). The policies enacted by the Hungarian leaders at that time to force these other communities to adopt Magyar linguistic, religious, and other cultural characteristics led to "racial [*sic*] tensions," "open conflict," and increased support for the Habsburg emperor by these minorities (Hoensch 1988:5). The conflict that was generated contributed to the defeat of the Hungarian nationalists in their war of independence against the Habsburgs in 1848–49.

The period of the War of Independence must be marked as the birth of Hungarian nationalism on a wide scale because it was the first time "the Hungarian peasant . . . saw in the Magyar landlord (whom he continued to hate and to distrust) a closer relative than in the non-Magyar speaking peasantry" (Sugar 1969:38). In addition, the chauvinism that had infected the nobility's Magyar nationalism from the beginning was taken up by the peasantry when the peasant classes of the national minorities were seen to side with their own leaders and the emperor in clashes with Magyar forces. It had taken more than eight hundred years, but at this time all sectors of Magyar Hungarian society betrayed the advice putatively given by their first Christian leader and patron saint, István, to accept and welcome foreigners into the country. Supposedly, István had claimed "a country unified in language and in customs is fragile and weak" (cited in Jászi 1961:39). Common sense, based on their experiences of the war, told many Magyars otherwise.

Throughout portions of the twentieth century, the Hungarian nation was as useful for legitimating a variety of political, social, and economic movements as it had been in the nineteenth. For example, following Hungary's defeat in World War I, the Treaty of Trianon divided up the territory of Greater Hungary and redistributed about two-thirds of it to the national groups who made up the majority population in each region. Transylvania, in eastern Hungary, was transferred to Romania; the Voivod in southeastern Hungary was transferred to what was then Yugoslavia; Slovakia was carved out of northern Hungary; and both Austria and Ukraine claimed small portions of formerly Hungarian territory. Hungarians, who felt they had been unfairly treated, flocked to a number of different fascist movements that promised to fight for the retrieval of this territory. These movements also employed a variety of national myths and images to legitimate themselves. One such movement, the Hungarian Turanian Society, was formed with the specific aim of "foster[ing] linguistic, ethnographic, and historical research into the Asiatic past of the Magyar people" (Janos 1982:274). A second movement that developed under the umbrella of Hungarian fascism was the pan-Europeanist, which posited national socialism was not a political force to bring Hungary closer to her Asian relatives but one that would unify the Continent and dominate the globe (Janos 1982:275). Both the Turanists and the pan-Europeanists acknowledged Hungarian roots in the East and the superiority of the West (Janos 1982:276). The third and dominant movement within the broad category of Hungarian fascism, Hungarism, was based on the premise that Hungary should look neither to the East nor the West for leadership, but should dominate the Carpatho-Danubian Great Fatherland on an equal footing with Germany in the West and Japan in the East (Janos 1982:277). Hungary's unique position was based on the fact of their being the only peoples of Asiatic origin to adopt Western culture and thus possess an ability "to mediate between East and West" (Janos 1982:276).

Like the interwar period, the period in Hungary from 1988, when the Hungarian Socialist Workers' Party reformed itself and replaced the aging János Kádár, through the mid-1990s was marked by a striving for national identity and legitimacy in the face of economic, political, and social changes. And, like this previous era, this more contemporary period witnessed the development of a number of movements looking to Hungary's Eastern roots and to the mythic history through which many Hungarians have learned to identify with these roots. The Szittyas, who claim Hungarians are "one of the world's oldest peoples" and "the first settlers in the Carpathian Basin" (Kisimre 1993:5) represent one such movement. Most mainstream politicians represent an opposing movement, one that advocates the entrance of Hungary into the western European community, rather than looking to historical, Eastern roots for national legitimacy.

For the bulk of the population, however, Hungary in the mid-1990s remained where she had always been, in a vulnerable position between East and West. Unlike the Hungarists of the 1930s, however, many of the Hungarians I met in Szeged could see very few benefits of their inevitable position. The identity of mediator and border guard was accepted with resignation but regret, in light of the historical precedents of this position, particularly the experiences of being conquered from the East three times (Barany 1969:260) and the West once. The Mongols invaded in the thirteenth century, the Ottoman Turks in the sixteenth, the Habsburgs in the eighteenth, and the Russians in the twentieth. Indeed, although most Hungarians speak with pride about the uniqueness of their national community and the accomplishments of its members, many also speak of their "national pessimism." I had innumerable conversations with Hungarians about the fact that Hungary has never had a successful revolution; it is the only country, besides Paraguay, with a national anthem highlighting the country's failures; and they have an extremely high suicide rate. It seems to me part of their national identity is a sense of pessimism and failure, despite many successes. When, in 1993–94, the people of Szeged referred to their city as the gateway to the Balkans, as protecting Hungary and Europe from foreigners coming from the east and south, and as an extremely insecure city in an insecure country, they were drawing on this historical background and the pessimism that they feel accompanies it.

Communist Citizenship

As I discussed earlier, the one period of time in the modern era when the nation was not an important legitimating idea in Hungary was the thirty-two-year period between 1956 and 1988. During this time, talk of the nation in Hungary was officially silenced and replaced by a discourse of the state. In line with the Socialist Workers' Party's statism, citizenship in the socialist state replaced membership in the nation as the most important mark of belonging in the Hungarian community. Nonetheless, because of its importance in defining Hungarian identity for this entire period and the significance in the early 1990s of opposing the identities and structures imposed during this period, I briefly address communist citizenship here.

Communist ideology generally is premised on the idea that everyone must work. In socialist Hungary, this ideology was codified by the state in Article Two of the constitution of 1949, which "define[d] Hungary as a 'state of workers and working peasantry'" (Helmreich 1957:83). In 1972, amendments to the constitution replaced the term "workers" with "citizens"; however, the right to work, which both guaranteed employment for those who desired it and forced it upon those who did not, remained as a central tenet of the state and its Socialist leadership. Work remained important to the state leadership because it was "seen as the most important social activity for the survival and evolution of society as well as for the formation of the individual and of communities. In this sense participation in socially organized work [was] a socio-economic necessity and a moral obligation" (Ferge 1979:89). This statement by a Hungarian, at least nominally Marxist, academic is important for two reasons. First, unlike Marxism proper, the author focuses on work as the path to both economic and moral participation in the state. Second, she defines "socially organized work," that is, work in the state farms, cooperatives, and industries managed by the socialist state, as the particular kind of work that was to define the Hungarian state and its citizens.

Of course, citizenship, as much as membership in the nation, is a gendered identity, and this was as true of socialist Hungary, which codified gender equality in the constitution, as of other, less officially egalitarian states. Indeed, the emphasis on socialized work in Hungary at that time contributed to a variety of differences between citizenship for women and men. For example, according to Hungarian law before 1990, women as citizens were not required to be independent wage-earners as long as there was somebody to provide for them (Ferge 1979:89). Therefore, "parasitism" was legal for Hungarian women after 1957; yet, membership in the moral community of citizens was contingent for everyone on participation in what the state defined as work.

While women were defined by law as different kinds of citizens than men, they also were marked as different from the male standard economically. Socially organized work in Hungary was supposed to provide a livelihood for those who participated in it. However, despite the fact that three-quarters of all women did become workers and wage-earners (Völgyes 1985:221), because most families needed women's income for survival (Vasary 1987), their incomes often were not high enough to provide women with any independence from their husbands. As a result, their inclusion in this community remained tenuous because of their inability to provide their own livelihood. In addition, the implementation of paid maternity leave was supposed to redefine "work" to include traditionally women's household chores and to acknowledge their utility for society as a whole (Ferge 1979:100). However, this newly recognized kind of work was accorded only "40% to 50% of the average salary of the cohort (young women)" (Ferge

1979:46), which was itself well below the average for men of the same age with similar experience. These payments did not provide a livelihood for women through socially defined work. Therefore, although many women took advantage of the three-year maternity leaves that were made available to them (Vasary 1987), in the long run, women did not benefit from the economic and social benefits accrued to socially organized work, i.e., full membership in the moral community of citizens.

Women's low salaries do not tell the whole story of the marginalization of their work and their insecure position as full citizens of the socialist state. Women also played very little part in the power structures at all levels of society in socialist Hungary. Michael Burawoy, a sociologist who spent two months working in a Hungarian firm, found that women were excluded from even the lowest level of decision making. In his particular machine shop the male operators, including himself, were given their norms and jobs and then left to themselves to finish, while many of the female operators were formed into a brigade with a male "boss" who told them exactly what to do, when to do it, and how (Burawoy 1988:218). There was one woman who was not a member of this brigade and was thus able to work on her own; however, she too was less than fully independent since she was forced to make coffee for the entire group (Burawoy 1988:218). When asked why they continued to work with such segregation and subordination the women replied that they had no choice. Burawoy concludes that in socialist Hungary, regardless of the official egalitarianism, "the division into women's jobs and men's jobs [was] always accompanied by some form of gender domination. If it [was]n't integral to the jobs, it [was] added" (Burawoy 1988:218). The fact that this was written forty years after full equality became the law in Hungary indicates the socialist system, based on communist ideology, was in reality nearly as male-dominated as our own capitalist system.

While some of this gender inequality came from the way that Hungarians implemented their own laws, it is also true that communist ideology itself provided few specific directives for correcting gender inequalities. Marx and Engels themselves saw no problem with a gendered division of labor that accorded more value to men's work than to women's. In the first chapter of *Capital*, Marx writes of the division of labor in the family as a natural relationship: "different kinds of labour . . . such as tilling the fields, tending the cattle, spinning, weaving and making clothes are already in their natural form social functions; for they are the functions of the family" (Marx 1977:171). Other early socialist and communist theorists, such as Rosa Luxemburg, Klara Zetkin, and August Bebel were more interested in inequalities between men and women, but even for them the issue was not gender but "the woman problem."

In the development of "real socialism" (Verdery 1991b), or socialism in practice in the U.S.S.R. and eastern and central Europe, one of the few concepts from these theoretical antecedents to have been wholly adopted is the idea of a natural division between the work of women and the work of men (Corrin 1994). Women in Hungary were driven to seek outside employment due to low wages and parasitism laws in effect until 1957 (Völgyes and Völgyes 1977:54), but it was taken for granted that women's jobs would be less well paid and grant less prestige. At the same time, women were expected to continue to perform all household and domestic chores and to bear children for Hungary (Kürti 1991:58). Pronatalism became an official state policy in 1958, the first year Hungary's mortality rate exceeded its birth rate (McIntyre 1985:274), and continued on the agenda until its dissolution in 1990. At the heart of communist ideologies of work are the ideas that women's work outside the home is only a supplement to men's earnings (Völgyes 1985) and that women will continue to perform household and domestic tasks, so the state does not have to become involved. Central to these ideas is a division between private and public, unwaged and waged work, family duty and work, all of which divide women's activities from men's, and activities that reproduce the family and the individual from activities that reproduce the state and its citizens.

While the socialist system did not entirely equalize the positions of women and men in Hungarian society, I conclude this section with a reminder that many women were able to work outside the home, go to university and trade schools, and represent other women in local and national government and organizations during that time period. The socialist system, for all its faults, was progressive in its attempts at opening up public life for women. And, as I learned when I spoke with many women who had grown up and raised families during these years, many women were very disappointed with the transition away from the system that had provided them with these opportunities.

Back to the Nation

As is evident in this chapter, the situation I experienced in Hungary in 1993–94, in which the nation was a prime legitimating concept of the new social-political-economic system, did not emerge out of nothing. The nation has a long history in Hungary, which allowed different political parties and leaders to use the idea to legitimate themselves and their agendas. Indeed, in the early to mid-1990s, to ignore the nation was to harken back to the communist system, which was something no party or leader wished to do, even the revamped and revitalized socialists. At the same time, the Hungarian nation was also an important (imagined) community to which many ordinary people ascribed as well.

In the following chapter I look at kinship and other associations maintained by some members of the Szeged community, holidays, commensality, and other features of daily life and discuss how these local ties and symbolic systems contributed to these residents' views of the national community.

CHAPTER 3

Local Networks, National Identities

Introduction

Before arriving in the field I had read dozens of ethnographies in which the anthropologist described his or her relationship with informants as one of fictive kinship. In these books the anthropologist becomes an honorary son or daughter in an informant's family, is always invited to family events, included in important holidays and rituals, and from these relationships and events receives his or her most important research data. Because of this ethnographic record, I assumed that by the end of my own first year in the field, if I hadn't achieved fictive kin status, at least I would be close enough to someone or some family to be invited to join in a Hungarian holiday celebration.

As the end of November 1993 approached I felt it was time to begin thinking about how I would spend the holidays. I made broad hints to the people I considered my friends about having nobody with whom I could celebrate. I talked about how difficult it was to be away from my own family at holiday time and how interested I was in learning about Hungarian Christmas traditions. However, no invitations came. By the first of December I was beginning to worry about my status as an anthropologist: Was I a bad fieldworker because nobody cared enough about me to invite me to their home for the holidays? Why hadn't anyone taken me in and made me fictive kin? How did these other anthropologists become so integrated into the networks, kin and otherwise, of their informants? I decided to become more active in my approach to learning about Hungarian relationships and their enactment in ritual settings when I learned December 4th is my name day. I invited three of my closest friends to join me for pizza. I knew that few Hungarians celebrated name days with any sort of public acknowledgment like

31

this but I hoped my unfamiliarity with the name day concept would amuse them and get them thinking about the upcoming Christmas holidays.

To my relief my three friends did like the idea, so the four of us arranged to meet at my favorite pizzeria. During the course of the evening, I asked them an assortment of questions about their own name day celebrations, their friends, and their holidays. I must admit I was taken aback by their responses. I learned that not only was I not getting Christmas invitations from any of them, but after months of talking, hanging out, and occasionally having dinner with them, they did not consider me their friend. I was somewhat reassured to learn that they did not consider each other friends either, and they'd known each other for years, but it was still quite disappointing to know I was merely an acquaintance. Since that time I have become much more familiar with the idea of friendship throughout Europe and realize that, regardless of the changes in Hungarian society throughout the 1990s, I should not have expected anything like friendship to have developed between us in only one short year. Friendship for most Hungarians is a relationship begun in childhood, nurtured throughout the lifecourse, and, hopefully, lasted a lifetime. Of course, it doesn't always work out that way, as the stories about friendship I collected illustrate, but this ideal still provides the framework within which friendship is understood and experienced by most Hungarians.

Despite my realization that I was going to be alone for Christmas, I was still interested in the ways Hungarians celebrate this holiday, so I asked about their observances anyway. They were all staying home with their most immediate family members and having a quiet night. When they asked about my plans, I tried to look as pitiful and lonely as possible, told them how much I was going to miss my own family and friends at the holidays, and then said I had no plans. Their response was an unequivocal assurance I would definitely be alone for Christmas, especially Holy Night, as Christmas Eve is called, because these are family-only events in Hungary.

I was skeptical as to whether everyone else whom I knew in Szeged would be so seemingly cold-hearted about what they'd said was the most important holiday of the year. That night I laughed off their response and then began asking everyone I knew about their plans. The answers I received did not conflict with the reactions of these first acquaintances, as I'd learned to call them. The couple to which I felt closest during most of my time in Szeged, Irén and Attila, said they would like to invite me to their house, but his parents would not like it; however, they did invite me to spend the 26th with them. Most other people did not even place the blame on someone else; non-family members just were not welcome on December 24th. One young woman was not inviting her fiancé over until the afternoon of the 25th, even though she knew his parents live in a city quite far from Szeged and he would be alone for the most important holiday of the year. Another recently married woman said her parents used to invite many of the foreign students from the medical school (where her father is a professor) to their home for Christmas, "because it isn't good to be alone on that day." But in the few years prior to

1993 they stopped doing this because of the cost, time, and effort of having all those extra people in the house. That year, her parents celebrated at home with her unmarried brother and maternal grandmother, who lives with her parents, and she remained at home with her new husband.

Finally, on December 22nd (after I had given up all hope of seeing what a Hungarian Christmas was like and had walked all over Szeged to find the ingredients to make myself a Christmas lasagna), the colleague of an acquaintance of mine invited me to join her and her extended family for Christmas Eve. This woman is one of eight children, which is rare in Hungary since most families are quite small, and many of her siblings, their children, and grandchildren were going to converge on this woman's eldest sister's apartment for the 24th. Most people I knew in Szeged spent that evening just with the people with whom they live, sometimes with the addition of a grandparent or grandparents, so this family was unique in a number of ways. Not only was it larger than most, but it had also maintained closer ties. I quickly agreed to join them and rejoiced that, anomalous or not, I was going to see a Hungarian Holy Night celebration.

Everything was lovely that evening. My new acquaintance and one of her sisters picked me up at 6:30 on a cold and snowy Christmas Eve and delivered me to their eldest sister's apartment, along with several of my acquaintance's nieces and nephews, before heading back out to pick up their mother. I entered the bustling apartment just as two of the nephews were being ushered into a bedroom to be scolded for a wrestling match that had turned into a real fight. The rest of the children were being pushed from the living room so the baby Jesus could come and bring the tree and gifts. In Hungary, as in some other European countries, the Santa Claus figure, Father Winter, comes on December 6th to fill children's shoes with candy and other small gifts, while the baby Jesus comes on Christmas Eve with the decorated tree and larger gifts.

While many of the adults were busy playing "Baby Jesus" in the living room, I sat at a table just outside the living room door with some of the older children to have a cold supper of batter-fried liver and potato salad. I also tried my best to keep the younger children from peeping through the keyhole to see the miracle of Christmas going on in the living room. I wasn't sure at the time I had succeeded, but from the children's reactions when the doors were finally thrown open I must have managed with at least a few of them. One small girl looked wondrously at the beautifully decorated tree sitting where previously there had been just a small, round table. Her eyes lit up with such a combination of amazement and joy that I was positive she was not aware it had all been staged by her aunts and uncles. Many of the older children were more skeptical but everyone helped to perpetuate the myth for the benefit of the few who did believe they were walking into a room filled with magic. Sharing in the children's joy helped dispel my initial discomfort with joining such a large group of strangers on their most important holiday, and more than made up for having to eat cold, fried pig's liver for my Christmas Eve dinner.

Before the children were allowed to tear into their pile of gifts, everyone sat down with a drink and a piece or two of special Christmas pastries, flaky pastry with walnut or poppy seed fillings. One of my acquaintance's sisters played Christmas carols on the piano while her two sons accompanied her on the cello and violin. Everyone was very surprised to see I knew the words to these songs, as it appeared from the way my lips moved with the music. They laughed very hard when I explained I had sung (very softly) in English. Finally, after the songs and a prayer, the children were set loose to rip open their gifts. Unlike in the U.S., where Christmas is an opportunity for adults to exchange gifts as much as for children to receive them, none of the adults at this event gave anything to one another. Likewise, the children did not give anything to their parents, aunts, uncles, or grandmother.

Indeed, as is to be expected, many Hungarian Christmas customs were very different from anything I had experienced in the United States or in Britain, where I had spent Christmas in 1990. For example, on December 14th I was invited to dinner with some acquaintances and offered to bring the ingredients to make Christmas cookies for dessert. I knew these people very well and they were already acquainted with my odd, U.S.-American custom of offering to bring something when they invited me over for a meal. Usually they declined my offer but the opportunity to try a new kind of dessert intrigued them enough to humor me just this once. Nonetheless, they were still a bit confused by the idea of baking Christmas cookies as early as December 14th; surely, they argued, anything baked that early would be stale by Christmas. I assured them we did not have to wait until Christmas to eat them, which, to them, meant they could not be considered Christmas cookies. I soon learned that instead of the end of November through the beginning of January being the "Christmas season," Hungarians only celebrate on the three days of Christmas, December 24th–26th. My acquaintances enjoyed the cookies but could not think of them as part of a holiday celebration, since the season had not begun.

Szeged itself seemed to begin preparing for Christmas a bit earlier than my acquaintances. For example, in early December, a large evergreen tree was erected in the fountain area of the main pedestrian square and temporary shopping booths were set up in the walkway in front of the city hall. Even these additions, however, were largely unrecognizable as having anything to do with the upcoming holiday, save the sign above the shopping booths that read "Happy Holidays." The tree was decorated with one small string of lights and six large, plastic ornaments while the shopping booths played nothing but English-language pop music and contained the same array of products available in the stores all year long. There was no Christmas music, no decorations aside from the large sign hanging outside the booths and the nearly bare tree, no real sign that Christmas was a community event at all. As my interviews with people about their celebrations later showed, this is indeed the case; Christmas is not a time for reaching out but for closing in.

This is not to say that my hostesses and hosts for Christmas Eve were anything but warm and welcoming. I was fortunate to find a group that was outside of the norm. Indeed, it was not the addition of a foreign anthropologist anyone found odd or annoying that evening but the addition of the ex-husband of my acquaintance's niece. Whereas everyone greeted me, encouraged me to eat, drink, and be merry, and actively included me in their holiday, this man was left alone to play with his two young children. Then, as soon as they had finished opening their packages and trying out the games and toys he had brought for them, he was hustled out the door. As he was leaving I asked him where he was going and he said to his parents' place, "because they are the only family I have left."

As this narrative begins to express, many aspects of life I take for granted as a member of my own culture, such as friendship, family, holidays, and other features of daily life, are experienced very differently in other places, are given different meanings, and encompass a different set of values. Even when things appear on their surface to follow similar patterns or have similar meanings, as would appear to be the case with Christmas, these similarities can mask tremendous differences. In part, that is the nature of the anthropological project: to discover the ways in which different cultures create different realities for their members. In this chapter I explore these traditionally "anthropological" topics in the context of postsocialist Hungary. In many ways this chapter will be the most familiar to students of anthropology and others acquainted with traditional ethnographic writing because of its focus on kinship and other associations, holidays, and the symbolic aspects of other daily affairs. In other ways, however, the chapter should strike readers as somewhat different. The reason for this is that these features of individual, personal lives show the ways experiences in local communities provide the conceptual framework through which abstract national communities can be imagined (Cohen 1996, 2000).

Networks and Associations

In this section I examine the networks and associations maintained by a number of different people as representative of the general trends I found with all of my acquaintances in Szeged. Unlike Carol Stack, who found that poverty and economic insecurity led to both intensive and extensive networking and mutual aid among urban African Americans (1974), I found in Szeged in the early and mid-1990s that increased economic insecurity contributed to a diminishing of people's social networks. Rather than as a source of aid, friends, acquaintances, distant relatives, and neighbors were seen to a certain degree as burdens to already strapped temporal and economic budgets. The people I know in Szeged were more like the working-class U.S.-Americans interviewed by Lillian Rubin, who said, "'It costs too much and besides it's too much trouble'—[these are] major reasons working-class women rarely look forward to entertaining at home" (1976:195–6). At the same time, Rubin says these U.S.-Americans enjoy big holidays at which they are joined by distant relatives, their neighbors play an important role in their lives, and people occasionally "stop to visit a friend . . . for an hour or so" if they are out and about (1976:196). None of these things can be said for many people in Szeged, Hungary, in 1993–94. During this period, holidays were small, quiet events people looked forward to merely for the opportunity to rest. Few people had maintained relationships with neighbors beyond simple greetings on the street. Few people answered in the affirmative to the question, "Do you have any friends?"

In some ways these responses were not unexpected. Before leaving for Hungary I had read Katalin Tausz's short article that explores "why community development still has to find a role in Hungary" (1990). She argues, as do many scholars who were familiar with the societies of socialist eastern and central Europe, Hungarians, "deprived from life-giving, genuine communities, [became] atomised, tired subjects [who] escaped," in Hungary's case, "into accumulating wealth" (1990:301). What did surprise me was the fact everyone in Szeged with whom I spoke agreed that their own networks, their own sense of local community, was much stronger during the socialist era than in the mid-1990s. It was the insecurities and fears of the transition, much more than the atomizing tendencies of "actually existing socialism," that caused a breakdown in the most personal communities: households, kin groups, friendship circles, colleagues, and acquaintances. Of course, part of this response can be attributed to nostalgia for a period without unemployment, steady diminishment in the standard of living, or random criminal acts. However, in addition to their descriptions of past events I also saw people's photographs of large family get-togethers, name-day celebrations, and Christmas parties. Prior to my arrival in Szeged, people did seem to be more involved in socializing with extended family members, acquaintances, colleagues, neighbors, and friends than when I was there.

Friendship: *Nincsen most már* (Not anymore)

In the time-use surveys I conducted in Szeged from July–December of 1993, in which thirty-two people recorded for me all of their activities for one week, only one in four people recorded spending time outside of work with someone whom they would consider an acquaintance and no one used the word for friend at all. While these numbers certainly do not represent any sort of statistically relevant sample, what they did for me at the time was help to put my Hungarian acquaintances' lives into context and begin to ask the right questions in my interviews and life histories.

Even though I had already determined Hungarians in Szeged spend far more time with their immediate family members than with anyone else, that they spend no time with friends and very little with acquaintances, including neighbors, still came as quite a surprise to me. I began to ask questions about people's friendships and soon found that few people in Szeged had any friends at all in 1993–94. One woman, Iluska, whose views on friends and connections is illustrative of the answers I received, stated, "One's own family is most important." Like many in Szeged, this thirty-eight-year-old librarian works two jobs to maintain an acceptable lifestyle for her family; in addition to her job in the county library she and her husband also sell Amway. They both feel they have no time for people because of this extra work. In addition, she is also very embittered because, as she said, "I thought I had friends but it turns out they are only acquaintances. A half year ago I would have given a different answer, because I thought I could rely on friends and colleagues, but they aren't interested in what we're doing and I'm not interested in what they're doing. Just family is important now." When I asked her to explain how this has affected their lives she said, "We're closed up now. We go home, lock the door, and rest."

A married man in his mid-thirties, Tibi, who has three children from two different marriages, also has been disappointed in his past connections with people. In fact, he cites "people" as his biggest disappointment: "You can't count on people now." Part of this response stems from the fact that when his son was quite young his first wife asked him to leave; "I thought I could count on my wife, but I was disappointed. Everyday I experience people letting me down." He believes that most old connections weren't strong enough to withstand the system change and that Hungarians in the early to mid-1990s had a very difficult time letting people into their inner circle. Unless he counts his wife as his friend, he says he has no one whom he regards as such.

I spent a considerable amount of time discussing friends and other associations with people in Szeged, trying to understand what people meant when they said they have no friends. The explanations I received did not vary much; in addition to the kind of disappointment cited by Tibi and Iluska, people also gave money, time, and general insecurity as their reasons for not maintaining friendships, and even some acquaintanceships, over the years. One man, a retired unskilled factory worker, said he and his wife "don't have friends now because it's too expensive to feed them, give drinks, dress nicely for company. Our pensions are too small for friends." This couple felt as if their other associations with people outside of their immediate family, such as colleagues, had likewise diminished in the 1990s. Ten years earlier, when he was working at the factory, he said they had often visited with some of his work mates and their families, and that he would occasionally go out with them after work. He explained to me, "Things were friendlier then because everyone wasn't so poor." His wife summed up their feelings by saying, "It's hard between people now because some get richer and richer, others poorer and poorer." He agreed.

When younger acquaintances of mine likewise cited money problems as their reason for not seeking out the company of people they used to think of as friends, or even acquaintances or colleagues, I explained the way some U.S.-Americans get around this problem is "potluck" suppers. I knew this practice would be rejected by most Hungarians (see Mucha 1993), but I thought this rather cosmopolitan group of university-educated acquaintances would have heard of this practice. I was wrong. They were as shocked and appalled at the idea as their parents or grandparents would have been. They could never invite people to their home and then ask them to bring something! The rule of hospitality in Hungary is that hosts and hostesses must provide everything and guests may not bring anything that could be mistaken as a sign you mistrust the host's or hostess's ability to provide for you.

Of course, it took a number of lessons before I finally figured out this rule. One day after I had been in Hungary for a number of months, a mistake on my part finally made clear the rules of hospitality. A woman I knew from a nearby village invited my anthropologist-friend and me to lunch. I automatically asked, "Can we bring something?", as I would have done in the same circumstances in the United States. I knew immediately from her reaction something was wrong. Had I used the wrong verb for "bring?", as often happened. She asked whom we would like to bring. Now I was really confused. "I don't know," I answered, "whom would you like us to bring?" This line of questioning went back and forth for a few seconds until, frustrated, we both hung up and I stepped out of the phone booth to try to explain to my friend what had happened. She was as baffled as I was but we figured we would ask about it when we went to lunch.

Lunch that weekend was fine and after we had been there for a number of hours I asked, trying to understand what had transpired between us on the telephone, why our hostess had wanted me to bring someone else. It turns out I had not used the wrong verb for bring, as I thought. I had asked if I could bring "something" but, because this is never done in Hungary, she assumed I meant to ask if I could bring "someone," which would be equally odd, I believe, but at least within the realm of possibilities. She was shocked that not only do U.S.-Americans ask this question of each other but that some people actually allow their guests to bring something and others have parties where the whole purpose is to have each guest or group of guests bring a major component of the food or drink. No, the potluck supper is not the key to saving Hungarian friendships in times of economic stress.

In addition to poverty, many people also claim they have no time for associations outside of their immediate families. One man said, "Everyone is rushing or hurrying, so there is no time to meet or to have people in." My hairstylist during much of my time in Szeged, a woman in her early fifties who had not taken a vacation in three years, said she preferred the past, "when families got together with cousins, aunts, uncles, everyone, for name days or for a pig slaughtering party. It wasn't like now when nobody has time." One woman who is home on child care leave with her two small children said she doesn't have any bad feelings toward people and would gladly see her friends from high school or college, but "it just doesn't happen. Things have changed." When I asked her with whom does she spend free time, her answer was "nobody." Her husband agreed; he said, with regard to himself and his former friends, "We don't meet with each other any more; there's no time." A former elementary school teacher who works for the state's social welfare system and who was a Socialist Workers' Party member for twenty-seven years, says she misses the get-togethers, meetings, and friends she had while in the party. She doesn't find the time or opportunity to see people like she did in the past and now has no one with whom she can just sit and talk. A woman who had grown up in Szeged in the 1960s says of her childhood, "You couldn't travel or see foreign films, but there was plenty to do. People did a lot more visiting and talking then. We had friends and other close connections. Not like now."

While most people cited these constraints to friendship, and even to maintaining ties to acquaintances and colleagues, a few people also pointed to the danger or insecurities of the postsocialist era to explain why many people have let these ties wither away. One woman in her early twenties who grew up in an area village but has lived in Szeged since high school, characterized Szeged as a direct and open city where people aren't suspicious of one another. In the mid-1990s, however, she said, "People are closing up because of the danger in the area." She found people less willing to take a chance and get to know strangers. My hairstylist in Hungary also found this to be the case. She said when she moved into her apartment building in the early 1970s everyone on her floor made a point of getting to know her; they all celebrated name days and New Year's Eve together for many years, as her large collection of photographs attested. When new people move in nowadays, she said, "we just greet them in the hall." Similarly, the old ties she had established with the other tenants on her floor have been cut. "We still speak in the hall or on the stairs, but we don't receive each other any more." A history professor at Szeged's university pointed to these insecurities and placed them in historical context. He said, "We don't invite friends into our lives as children or as adults. Maybe this is because we live in a transitional or temporary society." He continued, "Eastern Europe is different from western Europe because things are always happening, historically, people are always coming and going." His point was that it is difficult to develop ties to other people when their situation, as well as your own, is continuously changing. This has always been true in eastern Europe, he argued, but was especially true in the early and mid-1990s.

Unlike many of the people I know in Szeged, Iluska, the librarian, was almost as fascinated with my friendships as I was with her lack of them. I had often spoken with her of my best friend from university, with whom I continued to correspond weekly while living in Hungary. She was incredulous we had so much to say to one another. When she asked me what I wrote about I told her I wrote about Hungary, both the good and the bad, plus my plans for the future. I explained my friend sent me letters about her job, family, and a long-term illness. Iluska didn't believe me. She said she would never tell any kind of problem to anyone but her husband; if she did write letters to anyone, which she did not, she would only write about the good things, "obviously." The very idea of sharing something so personal with someone who is outside the immediate family circle was both ludicrous and slightly horrifying to her. Indeed, this is not a new phenomenon in Hungary, she said, but rather one that has been strengthened and reinforced by the insecurities of the current era. She argued that Hungarians have always been slow to develop very close bonds with people and the stress of the current era has just reinforced this trait in many people.

Near the end of my time in Hungary, I took an organized bus trip from Szeged to Paris, France. I thought this would be a nice opportunity to travel to western Europe with Hungarians, to see their reactions and how they differed from a previous bus trip I had taken eastwards to Istanbul. I also thought I could tour with the group during the week, giving me a chance to see Strasbourg and the Loire Valley, and then spend a long weekend with good friends who live in Paris. I didn't tell the group immediately of my plans, but after I became better acquainted with some of my traveling companions I told them I was going to stay with my friends in Paris rather than tour the city with the group. They, in turn, became very upset I would waste my time in Paris and miss the opportunity to see the sites. I explained I had not seen my friends for eleven months and this was going to be my last chance to do so for many more months. The more I spoke, however, the more I realized my reasons were meaningless to them. My argument that I had been to Paris several times before and seen most of the stops on their tour was countered with the fact that I had seen my friends before, and besides, I hadn't seen everything on their agenda. Going out of my way, spending money, and missing a chance to visit a few museums and sites, merely to visit friends (whom they probably assumed were acquaintances), was just never going to make sense to this group of Hungarians. They were as baffled by my priorities as my librarian acquaintance was by my letter writing.

I spoke about these and other experiences with many of my Hungarian acquaintances and quite a few wanted to understand, and to help me understand, the differences between their friendships and my own. We first discussed the fact that most "friendships" in the United States are relationships Hungarians would define differently, as acquaintances or colleagues. However, even given this difference in terminology, the associations U.S.-Americans seem to maintain with others outside their immediate families was something they wanted to understand. One Hungarian acquaintance of mine who had been to the United States thought maybe my country's large size has forced people to rely on friends and other non-kin more than in Hungary. "In the United States," he conjectured, "the great distances between family members force people to make other connections. In Hungary, you can get back home and to your family from anywhere in the country in a matter of hours. Therefore, friendships and other non-kin networks are quite weak." A woman, who grew up in Szeged but currently lives in a village with her husband and three children, hypothesized it is only the wealthy in the United States, like the Ewings from Dallas she said, who have friends. She assumed the poor and middle class have no time for or trust in friends, colleagues, or acquaintances, as in Hungary.

The one partial exception to this trend that I found in Szeged concerns the relationship between neighbors. While most people I spoke with were like my hairstylist in no longer socializing with their neighbors, a few people did continue to socialize and/or give or receive aid from one or two. For example, a young female student of mine had joined into a relationship with an elderly neighbor whereby she would help care for this woman, do some shopping for her, and the like, and when she passed away the young woman would inherit her apartment. Another older couple I know often hired their neighbor to perform yard work that was too difficult or heavy for them to do themselves. While this was strictly a market exchange, perhaps it is notable they hired their neighbor to do it instead of a total stranger. Despite these examples, however, I cannot say the neighbor relationship in Szeged is considerably different from the relationship between friends, acquaintances, or colleagues. Some people may have maintained ties with one or two neighbors, but on the whole this network was comparable to these others in its minimal importance for socializing, mutual aid, or any other purpose during the mid-1990s.

It was not my intention in this segment to compare U.S.-American ideas of friendship with those of my Hungarian acquaintances in Szeged. I included this discussion of my own experiences with friendship in Hungary and the U.S. only as a way of contextualizing my own biases and explaining some of the feelings I had while in the field. My real purpose was to allow my Hungarian acquaintances to speak about their social networks in the postsocialist era and, perhaps, to begin to answer Steven Sampson's question about "the problem of friendship" in postsocialist societies. The "problem," as Sampson expressed it, concerned the effect on utilitarian and even conspiratorial friendships "when one can get meat at the market instead of through contacts; when one can articulate political ideas in parliament instead of over a bottle of vodka in a deserted summer house; when friendship is emotional but not conspiratorial" (1991:19). In Szeged, the answer to this question in the mid-1990s seemed to be that friendships and other relationships had yet to find their emotional raison d'être.

Family and Relatives: *Tönkrement a család Magyarországon* (The family is ruined in Hungary)

In addition to very small and often nonexistent friendship circles, most people in Szeged have also limited their range of "socially effective bilateral kin" (Rosenberg and Anspach 1973:15) to only those people who are geographically, genealogically, and emotionally very near to themselves. I asked dozens of people, in all phases of life, to list for me members of their family, their relatives, and others with whom they might have biological or affinal (in-law) ties but whom they do not count in either of these categories. The answers I received indicate the Hungarian family, as it is understood in Szeged anyway, very much fits into "the open-choice perspective" presented by Parsons, Schneider, and others (Rosenberg and Anspach 1973:12). In other words, for Hungarians in Szeged in the mid-1990s, there was a great degree of "permissiveness in establishing and maintaining social relations with kin" (ibid). As a result, individuals, within the constraints of class, gender, ethnicity, and other criteria, were relatively free to choose their "socially effective kin." In this section I allow some of my Hungarian acquaintances to talk about the choices they made in the early and mid-1990s and how these might have compared with earlier time periods.

One female informant, a woman in her mid-thirties, told me she considered her two first cousins to be like sisters, and their parents, her maternal aunt and uncle, to be a second set of parents. When I expressed surprise at her expansion of the idea of the nuclear family to these more distant kin she said it was because as a child she had spent so much time with these relations. She counts all these people as members of her family while the category "relative" is reserved for those people with whom she has consanguineal, or blood, ties but fewer affective, or emotional, bonds. Individuals with whom she has consanguineal connections but no affective bonds are not included in either the family or relative category; they remain acquaintances. This woman is quite rare amongst the people I know in Szeged for her inclusion of people such as cousins, aunts, and uncles in her description of her family. Many people do not include even their own parents, siblings, or grandparents within this framework, placing them with cousins, aunts, uncles, and godparents in the category of relatives because they do not live together or see each other often.

When I asked people what constitutes a family, most of my informants said, "Feelings and worry make a family." Many limited it to the people they worry about on a daily basis. The librarian with no friends, who said her family is the basis of the only connections she had maintained in the mid-1990s, considered her family to be just her husband and two children. She regarded her mother, who lived in Szeged and with whom she visited weekly, a relative because they did not have daily contact.

A thirteen-year-old girl I met through her language teacher, whose parents are divorced and who resides with her mother, provides an interesting example of the family in Szeged. This girl did not consider her father to be a member of her family because he remarried and had children with his new wife. This was the case although they saw each other nearly every day and he paid for all her education expenses, including an extended trip to Canada. This girl, as well as everyone with whom I spoke about this kind of example, said, "Of course he's not part of her family. He has a new family now. That's where his real concern is." Most Hungarians with whom I spoke believed that, because he had another family and lived in a separate home from his first daughter, this daughter would not count him as a member of her family.

A man who now lives with his second wife and their two children explained the workings of Hungarian families to me this way: "Families only expand downwards. My parents include me, but I only consider my wife and two children in my family." I found it interesting he did not include a son from a previous marriage in his family because the boy resided with his mother. Another woman phrased it, "Once you're married, your siblings and parents become relatives." Whereas this woman believed it had always been this way in Hungary, others disagreed. My acquaintance who invited me to her Christmas celebration, a middle-aged woman who has never married and who has also maintained fairly close ties with many of her eight siblings, said, "Sunday lunch used to be the biggest/greatest time of the week because everyone, all the siblings, aunts, uncles, and cousins, would come together for a meal cooked by my mother. Now nobody has time for this kind of tradition. I see that my nieces and nephews and their children are missing out on family." A young woman who grew up in Szeged but whose mother came from a nearby village remembers many visits during her childhood to see her second cousins back in the village. They always celebrated name days with these relatives and, during the summer, spent weekends together in the village. When I asked her mother about these visits she said, "Yes, I used to have family there." It is significant to note her use of the past tense. These individuals had not left the village prior to 1994; rather, their Szeged relations no longer considered them family, in the mother's case, or relatives, in the daughter's case. In 1994, neither my acquaintance nor her mother had been to see these village relations for five years. "There's just no time," my acquaintance said. In addition, she was not planning on inviting them to her wedding because, as she explained, "The connection isn't strong enough any more."

Many people said to me when I asked about their families and relatives, "We've narrowed the family circle." A divorced man phrased it this way, "Family is ruined in Hungary because of stress, unemployment, alcohol, and insecurity." This statement may be an oversimplification of the entire situation in Hungary generally, and even in Szeged specifically. However, I spoke with enough people in Szeged to know that for many, regardless of their experiences, these are the terms with which they describe their families. The interesting part of these descriptions for me was the window they provided onto these Hungarians' understanding of the larger "family" of Magyar nationhood (see Cohen 1996). If some Hungarians experienced their "socially effective kin" ties as more selective than previously, perhaps they also understood their ties to the nation as being less binding and more a matter of choice.

Holidays: *Elég!* (Enough!)

In conjunction with this reduction or elimination of friendship circles and the closing of the category of family, holidays, as the ritual displays and enactments of these networks, also had become simple days of rest to be spent with the narrowest circle of family members rather than large, festive events open to all with whom people have some sort of familial or affective tie. All three types of holidays celebrated in Hungary prior to 1990, traditional, personal, and national, were in 1993–94 very small celebrations, if any took place at all. I witnessed more than a full calendar year of holidays in

Szeged in my seventeen months there and I spoke to dozens of people about their celebrations. Without fail they told me holidays just aren't the events they used to be; the celebration and hoopla have diminished. The reason for this is that people are too tired to make the effort (West 1994).

Traditional holidays, such as Christmas and Easter, were at one time in Hungary a ritual enactment of local community ties (see Fél and Hofer 1969). In 1993–94, these and other traditional holidays were limited to such a degree that most public displays disappeared and Hungarians preferred to remain at home with their most narrow family circle to enjoy the quiet and the time to relax. A man in his mid-forties, who has lived in Szeged for more than twenty years, spoke with me about his view of traditional holidays. He remembers these holidays with his parents as being big events, especially Christmas. He and his parents lived in an apartment in Budapest, away from all their other family members and relatives. Nevertheless, his mother liked to create holiday spirit by decorating the flat and by cooking and baking all their favorite things. Over the three days of Christmas they always got together with the other families who resided on the seventh floor of their apartment building, as well as with a few families from other floors. "It wasn't like it is today," he said as he showed me photographs of large Christmas parties he'd attended as a child and young man. One woman in her thirties thought maybe Christmas was more festive in the past because people weren't unemployed or worried they were going to lose their jobs in the new year. She herself was merely looking forward to three days away from the office in which she works from twelve to fourteen hours per day.

New Year's Eve, or Szilveszter, the name day for December 31st and the title by which the holiday is known, also used to be a widely celebrated night. Many people spoke of going out at midnight onto Széchenyi Square, the main pedestrian square in Szeged, to greet people, toast the New Year, and have fun. I know some people spent that night out on the town in 1993 because I heard their voices occasionally from my room, but no one I spoke with participated in these outdoor events. Many people had also warned me during the week prior to Szilveszter that I should be in by midnight. Everyone cited danger as the reason for staying home alone, visiting their parents, or attending a function with colleagues from work. In the past they would have done these things both before and after midnight, but as the year changed they would have been out on the square with the rest of Szeged, celebrating. As I had feared would happen with Christmas, no one had any room in their small, exclusive celebrations to include a foreign anthropologist as the year changed from 1993 to 1994. I wound up spending the evening playing Scrabble with a fellow anthropologist while my landlady sat downstairs by herself watching television. I tried to get myself invited in to join her but she told me she was going to bed early; I took the hint.

I received many of the same answers when I asked people about their Easter celebrations as I had with regard to their Christmas and New Year's holidays. I spoke with several men who as recently as three years earlier had participated in a village custom in which men visit their female relatives and girlfriends, sprinkle them with perfume or water and receive painted eggs, chocolate, or money in return. In 1990, one man had gone with his then-fiancée's male relatives to visit all the aunts, grandmothers, and female cousins in the family. Neither he nor his new in-laws have bothered since then. A young woman told me she liked the custom because she was able to see many of her (male) relatives who lived too far away to visit on a regular basis. Other women were glad the custom has disappeared, since they did not want to spend the day getting up to answer the door and then having to sit and visit with everyone, give them a drink and maybe a snack. On the whole, most people were glad to see an end to large Easter celebrations that cut into their three-day holiday weekend away from work and other responsibilities; the last thing most wanted, especially women, was to have the work of preparing for a large family event thrust upon them.

While traditional holidays ritually display and enact local community networks, personal holidays, such as name days and birthdays, display and enact personal networks (see Stone 1998:92–3). In 1993–94 these kinds of holidays were still sometimes observed by the closest family members in Szeged but rarely was there a celebration that included more distant relatives, friends, colleagues, or acquaintances. At the same time, while getting people to talk about their traditional holidays was not terribly difficult and I had some opportunities to experience them, getting information about personal holidays, such as birthdays and name days, was much more difficult. This is true, in part, because adults in Szeged do not tend to celebrate either of these days, as I said earlier about name days. They are considered children's days and as such are extremely private affairs. Even my closest acquaintances didn't invite me to their children's events, nor did they have much to say about them. The few examples I have of these events are thanks to my own birthdays in 1993 and 1996 and those of the other U.S.-American anthropologist I knew in Szeged. For both of us, birthday celebrations meant a special lunch made by our landladies.

In 1993, my birthday fell on what was the hottest day of August; the thermometer in the center of town read 45° Celsius, about 113° Fahrenheit. Despite the heat, my landlady made a beautiful three-course meal. We began with hot chicken soup, which is always served from three different pots, one for broth, one for vegetables, and one for meat. That day, since it was my birthday, I received the meat pot first and was told to take the chicken head and one of the feet, which had been boiled in the broth for most of the morning. I was pretty sure I didn't deserve the honor of eating the one head, primarily since I wasn't sure how to eat it, so I passed it on to my landlady's eager daughter, who immediately ate all the skin, including the comb, and then bit the top off the skull to suck out the brains. Having passed on the head because there was only one I couldn't really do the same with the feet, since there were two of them, so I took one of them and watched my landlady's husband devour the other. Following his lead, I sucked the skin off the foot and leg, nibbled on the connective tissue and fat pad at the bottom, and then gently set the claws onto my plate. Following the soup, my landlady served my favorite meal, chicken stew with paprika served over mini dumplings, and then several plates of pastry. Nothing, however, was as important as the chicken foot for creating a celebration. Unlike at birthday celebrations in the U.S., where the serving of the pastry, or birthday cake, is the primary celebratory moment with candles and singing, in Hungary the pastry was just a normal part of Sunday lunch. It turned out the serving of the chicken parts was the only moment when my birthday was acknowledged at all during that day.

My birthday in 1996, and those of my fellow anthropologist in February of 1993–94, also were celebrated with lunches. Neither of us ever received another chicken foot or head, but we also were not left alone on those days. I'm not sure how these celebrations compare with birthday observances in the past, but certainly my inability to experience more of them or to get people talking about these events is an indication of their unimportance in the early to mid-1990s.

In addition to these traditional and personal holidays, national holidays in Hungary, as the ritual display and enactment of the national community, were in 1993 and 1994 treated as just quiet days off from work. In the latter years of the socialist period, such national holidays as March 15th, which is the celebration of the War of Independence of 1848 and one of Hungary's most important national holidays, and August 20th, which is St. István's day and the celebration of the New Bread, were big events because they were not officially permitted or sponsored. Prior to 1990, the day commemorating the revolution of 1956, October 23rd, was also celebrated in Budapest and some of the other large cities, including Szeged. In 1993–94, all of these days simply provided a day off from work on which people stayed home to rest because, as my librarian acquaintance put it, "Holidays today are too emphasized, like in the Communist period, we're required to celebrate Hungarianness."

Another woman said, "It doesn't matter if the system changed, holidays today are still used as an opportunity for politics and speech making." Her cousin, who had been listening in on our conversation agreed; "It's enough!", she exclaimed. An employee at a local bank and her husband also spoke at length with me at the end of August 1993 about Hungary's national holidays. They had not done anything for the August 20th celebration because, as he said, "It's too political, like May 1st [May Day] was in the past." She added that Hungarians are too tired and anxious to make a holiday. He then explained what the two of them were trying to say. "Under Communism you *had* to attend these events and have a good time, so it's lost all its appeal now. Now everyone is too tired from working so much and is just glad for a day off. Nobody is thinking about the reason! Some rent a video, catch up on work, or get ahead. But they don't make a holiday because that just creates more work."

Another of my acquaintances thinks it will take twenty years for holidays to become festive again because right now "we don't know how to make holidays." He believes it will take that long for Hungarians to develop a pervasive holiday spirit and be proud enough of something to celebrate it. He himself does not even get these holidays off from work because he owns his own small business and must get the work done. A retired man who spends most of his days reading in the public library said, when asked about national holidays, "They are only good for party members; the rest of us are just glad not to work." When I explained I meant national holidays after the system change and not during the communist period he said it was the same; "Nothing has changed."

I must admit I, too, found Hungarian national holidays to be very political and agreed the omnipresent party speeches detracted from the fun. For example, in 1993 I attended the traditional August 20th celebration at an historical memorial park outside of Szeged. I found the few amusement park rides and other midway attractions, which had attracted relatively large crowds, were greatly outsized by huge tents set up by many of Hungary's political parties. A few people milled about each tent, gathering pins and other souvenirs. There were also poorly attended debates among many of these parties' leading national and local representatives, excluding those from the coalition-leading MDF who felt the holiday celebrating the New Bread and St. István was an inappropriate venue for political posturing. Of course, their refusal to attend and the statement they gave to explain it were as politically loaded as any of the speeches presented that day so they needn't have bothered staying away, but at least it made the event a few minutes shorter.

I had another disappointment in October 1993, when the one event in Szeged celebrating the 1956 revolution was a wreath-hanging ceremony at the city jail. Once again, the main draw of the ceremony was that each of the leading political parties sent a speaker. As with these other politico-holiday events, as I began to call them, few people were in attendance to hear the speech making. March 15th, which many said was the most "Hungarian" of the national holidays, was also a very quiet day in Szeged in 1993. The only celebration was a private military parade and concert on the grounds of a nearby border guard base, attended only by the guards and their guests. Everyone I knew chose to spend the day as they would any other weekend day or holiday break from work: resting or working at home.

In light of these previous experiences in Szeged I did not expect much from the events planned for March 15th, 1994. I knew the president, Árpád Göncz, the most popular politician in Hungary and leader of the opposition against the prime minister and his coalition, was giving a speech and there were going to be wreath-hangings at several sites in the city. I planned my day around these events but didn't have very high hopes for the celebrations. As it turned out, none of my previous experiences prepared me for what I saw. The crowds at the wreath-hangings in the morning were larger than usual. Booths selling Hungarian tricolored (red, white, green) ribbons, pins, and flags were being set up on the sidewalks adjacent to the pedestrian area in the middle of town. By the time the president emerged onto the balcony overlooking Klauzál Square, the city had filled with people. Several thousand Hungarians, all dressed up and wearing newly purchased tricolored ribbons, pushed their way into the square and its surrounding streets to hear the president speak about freedom and the importance of a free and independent press. I was amazed and spent many days after the event speaking with people about it and thinking about its importance.

Over the next few months I reached many different conclusions regarding the meaning of this aberration in what I had been experiencing as ordinary holiday celebrations, or the lack thereof. In part, the popularity of this event can be explained by President Göncz's celebrity and the fact many people in Szeged claim a personal relationship with him from his days as an English professor and translator at Szeged's university. This was true even when this "personal relationship" was, as one acquaintance explained, based solely on the fact he was once the colleague of his wife's former classmates. Nonetheless, despite this popularity and their "personal" connections, none of these people had attended an event seven months earlier at which I saw President Göncz speak. This celebration, an assembly on August 18th, 1993 for leaders from all of Hungary's nineteen counties, took place outdoors at an historical memorial park outside of Szeged. Despite the interesting setting and accompanying festivities, this event drew almost no visitors at all outside of individuals participating in the assembly and the small crafts fair that accompanied it. Clearly, something else was going on in March 1994 to differentiate it from President Göncz's other appearances in the Szeged area, as well as other national, traditional, and personal holidays in this seventeen-month period.

A second explanation for this event's popularity may have been that March 15th happened to be the first truly beautiful spring day in 1994 and, being a holiday, many people would have spent the day outside anyway. However, this also worked against some people attending since, as two of my acquaintances said, it was the first chance they'd had to work in their gardens and they did not want to take time away from them to bother with the president. Neither of these explanations really accounts for why the population of Szeged, apathetic to every national and traditional holiday I had witnessed in my fourteen months there, would suddenly show up for a holiday celebration that was apparently no more fun and no less political in nature than all the others they passed up during the year.

I propose that by looking back to the events leading to what Bruszt and Stark (1991) call the "unfettered elections" of 1990, the actions of those who celebrated in Szeged in 1994 become more clear. Prior to the 1990 elections and the dismantling of the socialist system, the 1989 reburial of Imre Nagy, hero of the 1956 revolution, and the first officially sanctioned celebration of October 23rd in that same year served as measures of the opposition's strength and legitimacy (Bruszt and Stark 1991:219). Through them the opposition was able to challenge openly the state's monopoly on public spectacle, since separate party and opposition events were given equal television time and media coverage. In the end, these holiday celebrations "brought about . . . the state's admission of failure" (Kürti 1990:8) and a change in government in the spring of 1990. As in 1990, the elections of 1994 were about a change in the status quo, since the revamped Socialist Party won an overwhelming majority. By supporting President Göncz with their presence and enthusiasm in 1994, the people of Szeged, like those in Budapest four and a half years earlier, were using the opportunity of the national holiday to speak out against the status quo. They used the event to demonstrate their "ability to challenge the regime," i.e., the coalition led by the extremely unpopular MDF, and call for an admission of failure from the government.

I offer a number of different justifications for this argument. First, for most of the four years prior to the 1994 elections, President Göncz stood in opposition to the ruling coalition in both a political and a symbolic sense. Politically, the president was in opposition to the right-of-center ruling coalition because of his membership in, and leadership of, the leading opposition party, the Alliance of Free Democrats (SzDSz). Symbolically, and perhaps more importantly, President Göncz was seen as standing his ground in 1992 when the coalition attempted to limit the newly won right to freedom of the press. When the government's harassment finally led to the "resignation" of several media leaders in the so-called "media war," President Göncz refused to sign their letters and thus to ratify the state's reappropriation of the media. Therefore, in March 1994 it was not only President Göncz's presence but also the topic of his speech, a free press, that represented opposition to the government as it stood at that time and the insecurities many felt they had generated with their policies.

My analysis is also supported by the outcome of those May 1994 elections in which the MDF platform was thoroughly rejected by voters in Szeged and all of Hungary. I also received letters from people in Szeged about their holiday celebrations after mid-1994 that support my thesis. I have been assured by a number of people that all national and traditional holidays between that time and the millicentennial events of 1996 were nothing but days off from work. The tremendous spirit that emerged in March 1994 has been dormant ever since, with the exception of some of the festivities in 1996 celebrating 1100 years of Hungarian nationhood. Rather than signifying a change in people's attitudes toward holidays and the local communities with which they would celebrate them, that one day served as a protest of the insecurities and dangers many Hungarians felt had emerged after the first free elections. Their participation in the event was a call for a second sweeping change in 1994, in much the same way holiday celebrations had been used by Hungarians in Budapest in 1988 and 1989 to call for the sweeping away of the old one-party system. It was not a movement toward more expanded local community ties, which would in turn suggest an expansion of the categories used to imagine the national community.

Other Features of Daily Life

Based on the statements and experiences of my Hungarian informants, I argue that in Szeged in 1993–94, people's networks of kin, friends, acquaintances, and colleagues were smaller and less cohesive than they were prior to the system change and their holidays were celebrated by smaller groups of people. In addition to speaking with people about their networks and experiencing a full range of social interactions, I found some other important ways this contraction of local communities and mistrust of individuals and groups outside of the most intimate, face-to-face ones are symbolized. My introduction to these phenomena came not through words, specifically, but rather through a series of communicative actions and symbols, combined with my preliminary attempts at using the Hungarian language. The episodes I draw upon are a series of communicative moments between some of my closest acquaintances in Szeged and me and provide just a small number of examples of the ways the Hungarians I met represent to themselves and others the limits of their personal communities. Taken by themselves each of these examples speaks only to individual preference but when viewed together they help to illustrate the frequent and often unconscious ways members of local networks and communities in Hungary expressed their desire for small networks of family and friends.

The first example I address concerns one of the most basic symbols of social relations: commensality, or food sharing. Mary Douglas argues in her classic essay on food as a code, "food categories . . . encode social events;" food symbolizes "different degrees of hierarchy, inclusion and exclusion, boundaries and transactions across boundaries" (1972:61). As such, food, and even more specifically, the events at which food is eaten, shared, and given away, provide good opportunities to understand the ways people see themselves in relation to others. Sharing food represents inclusion in a group, even if only a temporary one, at the same time withholding it represents exclusion.

As a general rule, Hungarians, like many Europeans, do not invite non-kin members to their homes to share a meal. I received invitations from some people to come for dinner or an occasional weekend lunch, but in most cases it was because someone wanted to teach me about Hungarian cooking, tell me about a Hungarian tradition, or learn something from me. When I asked my hostesses if they often get together with friends, acquaintances, or colleagues for a meal, without fail they all said no. This response was not entirely unexpected given my reading of some of the classic Hungarian ethnography (Fél and Hofer 1969), but I was surprised to learn that most Hungarians participated in no food sharing events of any kind. This is certainly true of their treatment of the preserves, syrups, and baked goods women made, often from the products of their gardens. While many small producers do sell raw fruit and vegetables, either at the outdoor market or to a wholesaler or market for resale, turning these raw ingredients into food products makes them more personal. As a result, homemade jams, syrups and other preserves, and cakes and pastries are rarely sold, traded, or given away to people outside of the domestic unit. Again, as with meals, occasionally I was given a jar of jam or piece of cake to take home with me after an interview since it was imagined that I could not bake or make preserves and did not have my mother or grandmother in the area to do it for me. When I asked the women who gave these gifts to me if they shared their products with neighbors, colleagues, friends, or acquaintances, they scoffed at the idea. Giving these products away to other Hungarians, like the giving of themselves in friendship, would allow people to enter into the invisible barrier they drew around all small familial communities to keep out strangers and the dangers they bring with them. Hungarians, especially women, maintain exclusive boundaries with their food sharing in the same way they do with their social lives and holiday celebrations.

Wedding celebrations also provide an interesting example of the conscious use of food in the demarcation of social boundaries in postsocialist Hungary. Young couples, in conjunction with their families, have to make decisions about what kind of invitations they are going to give to different people. While an invitation to the church and civil ceremonies indicates a degree of familiarity with the couple or one of the families, an invitation to the reception and its multi-course meal indicates a much closer bond. Invitations to this part of the wedding are seen by all as very special and meaningful, as I learned when I accompanied one of my language students to his secretary's wedding. Every Hungarian with whom I spoke about his invitation assured me that it was very uncommon and put my student under a great obligation to explain my presence to the families and financially compensate them for the extra guest. Later, when I was invited to an acquaintance's wedding and reception, she herself assured me that ordinarily an acquaintance like me would not be invited to the reception, but because I am U.S.-American she wanted to make sure I experienced a full Hungarian wedding event.

This full wedding event, whether it is held in a restaurant or under a tent in the center of a village, is a night-long affair with many ritualized foods, events, and even changes of clothes, which all take months to prepare. Even couples who hold their event in a restaurant don't have weddings that differ significantly from those described in the Hungarian village analyzed by Fél and Hofer (1969). These couples still must find people to prepare most of the meal at home, since the cost of having the restaurant actually prepare the food is prohibitive for most people. Some of the tasks that must be undertaken include rolling homemade noodles into spirals for the hen soup, baking dozens of plates of both sweet and savory finger foods and special wedding cakes and pastries, distilling homemade brandy and making wine or purchasing it along with beer and soft drinks, and killing a pig and/or a lamb for stew. Because of all this special planning, cooking, and preparing, invitations to the event are very important for communicating to people exactly where they stand in the couple's social universe. As was the case with holidays, friendship circles, and kin groups, wedding receptions in the mid-1990s were said by many to be smaller events than they had experienced in the 1970s and 1980s. Rather than limiting the cost of these events by serving a less traditional meal or less alcohol, the Hungarians I spoke with said it was preferable just to limit the number of invitations issued.

In addition to food symbols, another highly visible symbol of the nature of many Hungarians' associations with others is the importance people place on locks and keys (see West 1994). From my very first day in a Hungarian home I noticed the importance of the locked cupboard, gate, and door for the Hungarian owner. These locks and keys have a symbolic importance that far surpasses their practical function of keeping out thieves.

During my first week in Szeged, after moving from the prostitute motel, I stayed in a private room arranged for me by one of the local tourist offices. When I arrived the kind hostess showed me to my room, located next to her combination living and sleeping room, and the toilet and bath rooms, located next to the kitchen. I was given a key to my own room, which I found odd since it was the only guest room in the apartment and obviously my hostess had her own key to the room, but I accepted the key and pretended I understood the directions for its use. It wasn't until after she had left me alone in the room to unpack and I went to use the toilet, that I noticed keys hung from the lock of every single door in the apartment: the door to the kitchen, her room, and all six of the closets and cupboards in the entrance hall. I saw during my first night that the keys remained hanging from the locks both day and night. I was baffled. It was understandable a single woman who allowed strangers into her home on a daily basis would want to keep her own possessions under lock and key, but that didn't seem to be the point of these keys. The keys remained in the locks when she went out shopping or to sleep at night. If I had wanted access to her belongings all I would have had to do was turn the key and let myself in. No, either they were part of an interior design scheme with which I was unfamiliar, or the keys had some other meaning in Hungary I did not understand. Just in case, I left my own key hanging in the door for the entire time I stayed with her. I didn't want to cause a scene during my first week in the field!

Soon I forgot about the keys at this guest flat in the excitement of finding my first permanent home in Szeged. As I was moving my belongings into my room, my first landlady, Veronika, began showing me all the amenities she had to offer, describing them in the simplest way she knew how: a sturdy table at which to eat and do my work; shelf space; a gas heater with which I could control the temperature of my room; a piece of orange, faux fur tacked to the wall next to the bed for warmth; and, of course, a key to the room. I was relieved to learn this, due not so much to my landlady's curiosity but to that of the two middle-aged men who lived in the back rooms of the house. My relief, however, was short lived. In the next moment, after showing me how to use the key and warning me about these men, she showed me where in the hallway she wanted me to store it. So, I thought, I have been given this key and been warned to keep my room locked, but I am supposed to put it on a shelf right next to the door where anyone in the house has access to it. I was apprehensive. However, she then proceeded to show me how to lock and unlock her own door, through which I had to pass to use our shared kitchen, and where to put the key when I was finished: on a shelf next to her door, in full view of everyone. Throughout my time there I never did bother to use my own key and it remained on its shelf collecting dust; however, I did dutifully lock her room and stash the key next to the telephone every time I ventured through her always-locked door. Neither of us ever had any problems with these men, nor any other of the multitude of people who moved into and out of those back rooms during the four months I lived with her, although with each new tenant I was warned to lock my door. I always wondered if she likewise warned the other tenants to keep their doors locked because of the U.S.-American living in the front bedroom. I suspect so.

Although these two examples focus on internal space, that is, personal living space, locks and keys provide an important line of defense in maintaining external security as well. Everyone in Szeged who lives in a private home has a fence around his or her house and yard with a gate that usually is kept locked. One family with which I became very well acquainted is terribly concerned their front gate remain locked at all times. While everyone I know in Szeged is concerned about keeping their gate locked, this family's fears were expressed to me in more concrete terms than many others used. They cited the terrible crime and threat from vandals that could reach them if their gate was left unlocked for even one minute. Every time I visited them they would ask me if I'd remembered to lock their gate, even after a year had passed and I'd obviously learned to lock the gate every time. At the same time many residents of Szeged take their gate-locking seriously, many of them continuously contradict themselves by their behavior. For example, this very same family that warned me so often kept one of their front gate keys stored on a semi-permanent basis in the mailbox just inside the gate, so they could reach into it from the outside and let themselves into the courtyard. Any of the criminals or vandals they feared who happened to see them reach into the box could have done the same quite easily. It made about as much sense to me as my landlady's insistence on locking her door and leaving the key in plain sight.

Most homes also have a second line of defense against these criminals chained up just behind the fence: a loud, snarling, angry dog (see West 1994). In my year and a half in Szeged I never did become used to these dogs and their not-so-subtle way of announcing I was passing by their territory. I couldn't walk down a residential street without all the neighborhood dogs beginning to bark and snarl. The first one, of course, would startle me into nearly tripping on the uneven sidewalk or stepping out into the path of an oncoming vehicle. But after I recovered my composure from the initial fright, I would amuse myself by listening to the rapid spread of doggy disgruntlement. The barking would spread from the first dog to the immediate neighbors' dogs, and so on until I had awakened an entire block or more of dogs. Sometimes, on quiet evenings, I would walk home and hear dogs in the distance erupt in their angry yowls and chuckle to myself at the thought of some other startled pedestrian. Like the keys stored in mailboxes and in plain sight, however, these dogs likewise made little sense to me. Despite the angry

Szeged security guard without his chain.

sounds emanating from behind the gates, many of these dogs couldn't have stopped much crime, since, from the sound of the rattling chains, it was obvious they were not free to roam the yard or even approach the fence.

The apparent contradictions in these behaviors and attitudes eventually began to make sense as my language abilities grew and I was able to ask more questions. I learned it is not so much the objects themselves that are important but what they symbolize. The dogs, keys, and gates represent individual attempts at maintaining small, exclusive social networks. The best way for the most personal community, the household, to keep others out is to lock the doors. Possessing the ability to lock a door or cupboard provides the security of knowing the owner of the key is in control of the relationship between strangers and the contents, human or otherwise, of the locked space. When I eventually asked my landlady about the locks and keys she said they were necessary because of the danger posed by criminals. I pointed out that these potential criminals could reach the key on the shelf as well as I could and she reminded me the locked door to her room sat behind the locked front door to the house and the locked gate to the yard. Only the two of us had all three keys, since the people in the back rooms used their own entrance, so I was safe. I received a similar answer from people who kept their dogs chained up in their yards; they just felt safer knowing the dog was there. Ownership of the keys and dogs were the main issue for these people, as well as many others who kept their dogs chained up and their doors, cupboards, and gates locked with the keys in plain sight.

Conclusion

By exploring personal networks and ties, that is, the ways in which the most local of communities are experienced, we gain a window to the ways members of these communities imagine the larger, national community. Thus, the increasingly constricted nature of life within local networks and communities in Szeged in 1993–94 affected the ways these particular Hungarians imagined community life at the national level as well. In the following chapter, I look at the way garden work and discourse provided another set of experiences for Hungarians in Szeged to use in imagining the national community.

CHAPTER 4

Hungary as a Nation of Gardeners

Introduction

From the moment I entered Hungary in January 1993 on an eastbound train from Austria to Budapest until I left the country a year and a half later, I was acutely aware that I was living in a very agricultural area. That first train ride took me through miles of rolling hills and harvested grain fields. Peering out of the taxi from Budapest to Szeged, I saw nothing but empty fields in which the following spring and summer grew sunflowers, corn, hay, straw, and paprika peppers. All of the houses in which I resided had fruit trees and vegetables growing in the yard rather than ornamental shrubbery and grass. Some of my first conversations with Hungarians revealed that small-scale agricultural production remains a part of many people's lives, whether they have lived their entire lives in Szeged, in Budapest, or in the tiniest Alföld village. Throughout my year and a half in Hungary, I spoke with many people concerning gardens, land, and agriculture and, eventually, helped a few people work in their gardens. As I soon discovered, producing something on the land is important to Hungarians of all class, educational, and occupational backgrounds. As it has been since the eighteenth century, working the land is an important part of what makes Hungarians "Hungarian" in their own minds.

Common territory is very important in most, if not all, national ideologies (Hertz cited in Sahlins 1989). For many Hungarians this is certainly true, as the large number of maps of "Greater Hungary," Hungary prior to Trianon, hanging in public buildings and private homes attests. However, I argue land, even more than national territory, was an important measure of what it meant for many to be Hungarian in the latter half of the twentieth century. Some evidence of the importance of agricultural work in the way many people imagined their nation comes from the criticism of Roma made by some

57

Hungarians. This population, which in Hungary saw themselves in opposition to the peasant worldview of their neighbors (see Stewart 1993:194–5), was in turn judged by these neighbors "against peasant ideals. . . . They [were] not often seen doing agricultural labor or keeping up gardens" (Bell 1984:294). For further evidence of the importance of land, as opposed to territory, I turn back to the historical view of national identity I presented in chapter 2. Part of the reason the Hungarian Socialist Workers' Party was seen as alien to many Hungarians was that it changed "traditional" land use patterns. During the socialist period Hungary did not lose any territory to foreign states, but relationships between individuals and the land changed drastically. By 1976 more than fifty percent of the population resided in urban areas (Völgyes 1980:113). The small number of people who remained in the countryside and continued to work primarily in agriculture, about twenty-two percent (Völgyes 1980), went to work for the state farms or local cooperatives; they were proletarianized. By taking away their ability to work the land in the ways custom had defined as national, in addition to numerous other anti-Hungarian actions, the party became the enemy of the nation (see Vasary 1987, 1990).

Tradition, however, was soon reinvented by people outside of the state leadership structure, who challenged the party and state for the right to define a moral community of Hungarians. In this struggle to define their moral community as national, rather than statist as was desired by the party, Hungarians reinvented their relationship to the land. Small hobby gardens worked by both urban and rural proletarians became as symbolically important in the creation of the nation as they were in the production of a continuous food surplus. These gardens came to represent the Hungarian nation in the socialist era by allowing people to think of themselves as participating in peasant modes of labor (Vasary 1990:172). The experience of working the gardens produced a face-to-face community of part-time cultivators engaged in the production of fruit and vegetables and an imagined community of Hungarians engaged in the continuation of the nation's agricultural traditions.

In the years between 1989 and 1994, most of the institutions developed during forty years of socialism were eliminated or greatly modified. One institution, however, that not only remained but took on even more importance than during the socialist period is the system of small, intensively gardened plots that surround Hungary's larger cities. These plots provided Hungarians with several different resources in the early and mid-1990s, including hours of enjoyment, fruit, vegetables, and eggs. Just as important, they served as an important element in the complex system of symbols, institutions, values, and activities many Hungarians use to define their national identity. During my time in Hungary I lived in one of its five largest cities, yet a significant number of my acquaintances produced much of their own fruit and vegetables on these small privately held plots of land. When I began to ask questions about these hobby gardens, I found privately held gardens were used by many people in Szeged to discuss important aspects of themselves as individuals and of the nation as a whole. Indeed, this was true regardless of whether people owned a garden or even enjoyed working in one. At the same time, they also used them to talk about security.

One of the clearest statements I received with regard to the symbolic importance of these gardens came from a woman in her late twenties, born and raised in Szeged by parents who continue to work their plot intensively, but who, like many young people, did not yet want to work one herself. She said, "If we didn't have these gardens, we wouldn't have bread." When she and I had this conversation I had already been living in Szeged for nearly ten months and had learned the value of bread to Hungarians. For example, when many Hungarians measured the insecurity of the economic system in the early 1990s they did so by citing the cost of bread in different time periods. If I heard it once, I must have heard it a dozen times that bread in 1988 cost 3.6 forints a kilogram (when I arrived in 1993 it was sixty forints and eventually reached one hundred). I had also heard from many older informants that there is a mystical connection among land, wheat, and bread for Hungarians, and that bread equals life. Therefore, by relating hobby gardens to bread, even though these gardens in the Szeged area are never used for the production of grains, this woman provided me with an important connection between different conceptions of the Hungarian nation. The importance of land and agricultural work had been combined with a contemporary focus on security and was being played out every time someone weeded a row of peas, picked a bucket of cherries, or even talked about how they didn't need a garden because their life was already secure.

Andi and Sanyi enjoying a day in the garden.

Much like the almost universal importance of territory in the imagining of the national community, working the land is also an important characteristic of many European nations. For example, many people who have written on the British version of Hungary's hobby garden, the allotment, have made the claim that "the British are a nation of garden lovers" (see Thorpe 1975:169). In Denmark, France, Germany, Greece, and the Netherlands allotments also are popular (Lawson 1994:44) and in each country take on a different cultural identity. In many other countries in eastern and central Europe as well, working in private gardens has taken on a practical importance in the postsocialist era, when inflation, unemployment, and other aspects of "structural adjustment" have made gardening an important part of both self-provisioning and household income (Creed 1998). My point in this chapter is not that this is a unique aspect of Hungarian society or identity, but rather it is a very important aspect and, at the same time, in the early and mid-1990s, was discursively connected to people's feelings of insecurity.

In this chapter I tell the stories of four different people from Szeged to show the ways gardening and security were combined in interesting and constructive ways in the minds of both garden owners and non-owners. I have chosen these four over the many other Hungarians I met because I believe their stories represent a good cross-section of Hungarian life in Szeged: men and women, old and young, married and single, relatively well-off and struggling economically, intellectuals and blue-collar workers, garden owners and non-owners. Through their stories I show that even today many urban Hungarians continue to use their local experiences on their plots to imagine the character of the nation as a whole. As one forty-two-year-old garden owner said to me when I asked him to describe Hungarians, "Agriculture is the most important thing to us because Hungary is not an industrial nation. Agriculture connects people to each other." While most people in Szeged have only the most peripheral relationship to agriculture itself, many connected gardening activities with the positive values they attributed to it. As both an activity and a symbol, gardening serves for many Hungarians as a primary building block of the Hungarian nation.

Case Studies: "During times of instability it is better to live closer to the land"

Viki

Viki is in her mid-twenties and lives at home with her mother and younger sibling. Viki herself has a university degree and her family can be classified as intelligentsia. Her father was a surgeon before his death; her mother was a college professor and had published extensively in her field before her retirement due to ill health; and her sibling is at university. The three of them live in a large, four-room apartment in the city center that they rent from the city council. The family first had access to such a prime apartment because Viki's paternal grandfather was well placed within the Communist Party. Their fear when I was there was that after 1994, when Viki's sibling marries and leaves the family home, they would be unable to keep such a large apartment. They hope to be able to hold on to it by taking a boarder or two.

Money is a perpetual problem for this family. During my time in Szeged they were forced to sell their car and Viki's mother had gone into business, privately selling health and beauty aids along the lines of a U.S.-American Avon lady. After graduating from the university in Szeged, Viki has remained there, teaching part-time and doing administrative work in the department in which she took her degree. She turns half of her small salary over to her mother for her share of the rent and utility payments and, after putting a little aside for furniture and other things she will need when she marries, the equivalent of about ten U.S. dollars per month remain for all of her personal expenses.

I spent more than fifty structured hours with Viki conducting interviews, gathering her life history, and talking about life. We also spent countless more unstructured hours together during which her boyfriend, mother, and/or sibling were often present. In addition to her hopes and dreams for the future, Viki also told me about her childhood, of growing up in a household where they read books, went to concerts, watched television, and discussed current issues. She contrasted these activities with workers' families, where one or both parents go to a pub after work and the children spend their evenings alone, as well as with village families, where there isn't anything to do or discuss except the care and feeding of chickens and pigs. Rather than with pride or superiority, she told me these stories with a sense of gratitude that she was able to benefit from her background in ways others have not been able to do. She hopes that if and when she has a family of her own she will be able to provide the kind of education and experiences she herself had. She is afraid inflation has made this nearly impossible but hasn't given up that prospect.

Despite this intellectual background and a desire to pass this lifestyle on to any future children she may have, Viki spends much of her free time during the spring, summer, and autumn working in a garden, dividing her time between the family plot and her own personal one. The family garden, which can be reached from Szeged by bus followed by a hefty walk, was purchased by Viki's maternal grandfather in the 1970s at the cost of half an average month's salary. At that same time, her grandfather also erected on the property a small, two-room house, a separate summer kitchen, a chicken coop, an outdoor fireplace, and an outhouse. In addition to these structures the plot holds a number of fruit trees, including sour cherries, apricots, and peaches, a large grape arbor, a shade tree with a swing underneath it, and a small plot for growing flowers. Although most time spent at the garden is devoted to work, this garden spot also provides Viki, and occasionally her mother as well, with a relaxing place to come during the summer to escape the dirt, noise, and heat of the city and their sixth-story apartment. Occasionally

Viki's boyfriend is also invited to share a meal cooked in a kettle over the outdoor fire or just to play cards around the table inside, during which even her reluctant sibling can be coerced into joining them. Usually, however, Viki goes to the garden alone.

If I dropped by the garden unannounced when Viki and/or her mother were there, the radio would be on, the family dog would be chasing birds and cats, and whoever was there would be on her knees hard at work pulling weeds or halfway up a tree dropping cherries into a bucket. At these times they would always have time to stop and talk for a few minutes, but after a short break we'd all go back to work. The hardest task I had at these times was convincing them I really wanted to help and that I enjoyed risking my neck to reach more cherries than anyone else (being many inches taller than anyone in their family gave me a tremendous advantage!). It is very unusual in Hungary for a non-family member to work in a garden at a task the owner or owner's family members could do themselves. Like the sharing of food discussed in the previous chapter, garden work helps to define people's primary units of production and consumption. Occasionally an expert may be hired, or someone with the proper tools may be engaged to take down a tree, improve drainage, or put up a fence, as happened when half of Viki's family's garden was trampled by dogs that had gotten in through a hole in the fence in July 1993. However, these are rare events and the services are always paid for. I worked with two sets of acquaintances in their gardens during my time in Hungary and every time I did so I was inundated with enough fruit, syrup, jam, and vegetables to feed me for days; usually I was also given a large lunch or dinner. Despite my protests that I enjoyed the work, wanted to help them, and wanted to learn something about Hungarian gardening, they felt the need to pay me in produce for my efforts. I believe by the time they fed me and sent me home with baskets of ripe fruit they probably would have been better off to let what I picked go to the birds or rot off the trees.

For a variety of reasons, Viki regrets her family did not have the foresight or ability, she's not sure which, in the 1970s to purchase more than one of these plots. The plot of land her grandfather bought for half a month's salary would have sold in 1994 for half a year's wages or more. She feels this way even though she would have wound up tending both plots, in addition to her own, since her sibling has no interest in working the garden while at university and her mother's health prevents her from spending much time in the heat and dust. In addition to the relaxation time, Viki says she values the ability to provide fruit and flowers for herself and her family and more plots would have meant a greater yield at picking time.

During the summer when Viki is not at the family garden she is working with the fruit trees on her own small plot of land. Her father had hoped to leave both of his children a plot of their own but was unable to do so before he passed away. Unlike the family plot, Viki's own garden contains only a small tool shed and is not used for recreation; it is solely a work place. Her priority in the fall of 1993, when she had a little extra money from the sale of a particularly large peach crop, was to put in six more fruit trees rather than to expand or improve the building on the site. She said because she is a single woman she isn't able to make any structural changes to the land to make it into a real hobby garden, but she could probably get her sibling to help in the planting of the six new trees. She hopes the sale of the extra fruit from the new trees will allow her to have a small house built on the plot.

When I asked Viki to describe the different urban Hungarian gardens and how she would classify her own, she explained that unlike earlier in the history of the hobby gardens, in the mid-1990s there were both working and resting gardens, that is, gardens used primarily for leisure purposes. She was even able to cite examples of individuals from Szeged who bought plots from people who needed the money and then hired others to tend them while they themselves merely enjoyed the peaceful spot away from the city, an unheard-of practice until two or three years earlier. In her own case, she feels that like most, their family garden is a combination of the two; the family enjoys it as a garden and as a recreation area. Her own garden, however, more closely approximates the gardens of the late 1960s and 1970s; her pleasure in it comes from the work and the produce rather than the spot itself. Like people in the generations before her, Viki hopes to be able to erect proper buildings on her own garden someday, but even when she reaches this goal she wants to continue to grow her own fruit and flowers. She explained that she grows luxury items rather than potatoes or carrots, because her family will always buy these staples in the market but if money is tight then fruit and flowers are not part of the daily budget.

Zoli

Zoli, who was in his late sixties when I was in Hungary, is retired from his job with the state railway and lives in a garden house, that is, a single family home with a small yard or garden, in Szeged. He lives with his wife Éva, who, at sixty years old, is also officially retired from the railway but in 1993–94 continued to work more than forty hours per week at a private firm. They have two adult children, one living in an apartment very near to the family home and the other living in a smaller city north of Szeged. Both children work full-time, but, like many young people in Hungary, they could not support themselves without their parents' help. In fact, the reason given for Éva continuing to work is that neither child can make it from month to month on his or her own salary.

Like Viki's family, Zoli is extremely well-read and had even completed two years of training to become a pastor before the Communist Party took over Hungary in 1948 and changed his life forever. Whenever I went to visit Zoli he always had some new book to show me, or an old map depicting Hungary before the Treaty of Trianon, or a painting by his favorite local artist, or textbooks of his from the 1930s, or old family photographs. He is interested in everything, even to the extent that he often sits in front of the English-language news broadcast the cable television system brings into his living room twenty-four hours per day, despite the fact that he doesn't understand a word of it. Often he would have questions for me: What does this word mean? Why does the newscaster's tongue stick out when she says certain words? How do I say this or that in English? Despite this curiosity and desire for knowledge, Zoli was never allowed to complete his university or vocational education because the party discriminated against him for having been affiliated with the Hungarian Reformed Church. He began several different courses of study, including veterinary science, but when the party learned of his past he was always removed from the school. He cites his inability to become a pastor as his greatest disappointment and at first found it very difficult to have to work with his hands after having completed a degree at an academic high school. But in the mid-1950s a colleague introduced him to the small blonde woman whom he'd seen so often in the company canteen and they've been together ever since. They've built a house, raised two university-educated children, and live quite well by Hungarian standards. Zoli is a fascinating person and I owe much of what I know about Szeged, Hungary, and the Hungarian language to him.

In addition to all of his intellectual interests, such as reading history, studying art, and maintaining his fluency in German, Zoli loves to care for his chickens and work his three plots of land. He and his wife have a half dozen fruit trees, gooseberry and raspberry bushes, a small patch of vegetables and more than a dozen chickens at home, plus two different hobby gardens outside of Szeged. The first one, purchased in the early 1970s, was their primary weekend spot when the children were growing up. While there they tended to the trees and grapes, enjoyed the fresh air, and visited with Éva's sister's family, who has a garden in the same area. They spent many nights when the children were growing up in the small house on this plot of land, though by 1994 no one had slept there in quite a few years. During the summer of 1993, this home stood unused for all but one afternoon, when Zoli and Éva invited me to lunch. The second, larger garden with its small house was bought from a colleague in the mid-1980s, after his wife passed away and he could no longer work the land effectively. The porch of this garden's home is used each weekend in the summer to rest during a long afternoon of picking or watering, but, like the first one, the house itself is nothing more than a storage area for tools and extra furniture. Despite this, Zoli spends a great deal of time working on both houses, maintaining the roof, rewiring, and updating the plumbing.

The fact that Zoli and his wife have two gardens, in addition to living in a garden home, makes them a bit anomalous in Szeged. Many of my acquaintances told me that if somebody has a family house with a little land around it then they won't have a hobby garden; these gardens are owned by people who live in the large apartment communities that ring the city. I was also told that to have two of these gardens was somewhat risky during the socialist era because if the party noticed you could afford them they would take one or both away. In the postsocialist context it is considered ostentatious to live in a private home and hold two other pieces of property when so many people cannot afford the rent on even a small apartment without taking a second or third job. Zoli scoffed at these ideas and said people who say them are envious and lazy.

At least three times per week during the spring and summer Zoli takes the car and spends a portion of the day at one or the other of these gardens, weeding, watering, performing some other chore in the house or garden, or simply resting. Occasionally he hires a neighbor to help spray pesticides, build a fence, or take down a tree because his own health prevents him from such heavy work. Every evening he finishes his share of the work and sits down to rest at about the time Éva comes home from her paid job, whereupon her share of the garden-related work is just beginning. She spends almost every evening in the spring and summer planting seeds or seedlings in pots on the back terrace, weeding rows of young plants that have yet to be transferred to the larger garden from the backyard, or washing, pitting, or otherwise preparing the produce Zoli picked that day. Between making dinner and taking care of her share of the garden work, Éva does not enjoy a free moment on summer evenings (with the exception of one hour on Fridays to watch *Dallas*). On weekends during the summer, one entire day is always devoted to the larger of the two gardens. They pick, weed, water, and otherwise work in the garden, interspersed with several rest periods to have coffee, soda water, and fresh fruit. And then each evening, after a quick weekend meal, Zoli has a long rest to look forward to while Éva again spends the evening making jam or preserving fruit or making fruit syrups.

During the summer of 1993 I accompanied Zoli and Éva to their garden whenever I had a free Saturday, and whenever I could convince them I really wanted to help. Neither of their own children really enjoys working in the garden, though the one who lives near home does help out when asked, so I had a difficult time explaining why I wanted to spend an entire Saturday working outdoors in the middle of nowhere (or, as Zoli would say with a chuckle, behind the back of God). Garden work is considered very difficult and it was only when I explained that I needed a break from the city and mental work that they began to understand my desire to accompany them and engage in physical labor. Many other garden owners with whom I spoke about this issue also found it odd to have a "stranger" working in their garden. In fact, the only people who allowed me to help were Zoli and his wife, after many weeks of badgering them, and Viki, on the few times I happened to catch her working at the garden and could convince her I really wanted to help.

For Zoli and Éva, working in the garden is not just a hobby or something they do to relax or for the thrill of growing a few salad ingredients; working in their gardens is something they do because they feel they have to. Economically, they feel obligated to work in the gardens because their children need financial help and Zoli's health prevents him from working for someone else. When I asked why they don't pursue some other, easier, informal economy work, I was told they own the land anyway so it is best to use it. Morally they are obligated to work in the gardens because the land they own cannot be allowed to sit empty. When I asked Zoli why he took on the extra garden at a time when ill health forced him to retire from his first job, he replied that there are two of them who can get the work done while the former owner is a widower. The garden was extraneous for him and was going to sit unused, which would be a shame.

For Zoli the second, larger garden represents a way to keep active even though he has been denied the possibility of formal employment for medical reasons, as well as the ability to leave a garden to each of his children eventually. When I asked him why Éva would want to double her workload with the extra garden, Zoli replied that she is a little crazy and wouldn't be happy without work to fill her time. When I asked Éva the same question, she replied she needs to work hard because her children's salaries aren't enough to live on; besides, she said, she has always worked and wouldn't know what to do if she weren't busy all the time. Despite their years of employment in the state sector and, for Zoli, an urban, industrial family background, both Zoli and Éva feel a moral obligation to work the land.

Lajos

Lajos is in his mid-thirties, married, with three children between the ages of three and twelve. The family lives in a publicly subsidized apartment in central Szeged, rented to families with low incomes and several children. This is very important because the family has no car and cannot afford frequent journeys by bus or tram. They had only recently been allowed to rent this particular apartment when I met them, due to their low income and three children. Before this time, they had been forced to live in a dilapidated, cockroach-infested, two-room apartment because of its convenient location and affordable rent. Márta, Lajos's wife, is home on child care leave while Lajos works part-time at a number of different jobs: salesman, technician, photographer, and just after I met him, he established his own firm to make greeting cards. He received some technical training while working for the local tram company and has also trained himself in photography and computers. Márta completed half a year of teacher training school before leaving to have their first child. This family is probably the poorest I met in Hungary and is forced to live with the fewest comforts. Empty yogurt containers double as their drinking cups and only four people at one time can eat anything requiring a plate. What little furniture they have is old and falling apart. The eldest child sleeps in the small, unheated pantry off the kitchen. There is no refrigerator or television in the apartment. During the week I returned to the United States in July 1994 Lajos learned that he had been laid off from his latest position and they were waiting to see how his card business would do. Márta has discussed going to work, perhaps at a day care center or nursery school, but found every place wanted someone with a certificate or degree in child care. She doesn't know what she will do when her benefits run out and financially she is forced to work outside the home.

Besides their poverty, this family is also unique amongst my acquaintances in Szeged for their strict vegetarianism. Lajos said that when he was in his early twenties he and some friends began exploring Eastern religions and ever since then he has been a vegetarian; Márta became a vegetarian when she married Lajos. In addition to their vegetarianism, other signs of their religion are visible in the house. In one room there is a small table with incense and a small statue of Shiva on it, above which hangs a wall hanging with scenes of Indian life, and numerous books on the life of the Buddha are visible on a book shelf. Lajos and Márta have also told me of the first years of their married life when they lived on a self-sufficient commune with other practitioners of their Eastern religion and of the visits to Szeged of a famous Yogi.

In addition to his religious beliefs, land is also very important in the construction of Lajos's identity. The first thing he said when I asked him to tell me about himself was that his family is *törzs gyökeres Szegedi*. Literally, this phrase means "having tribal roots in Szeged," but when people use it today they mean that all ancestors the current generations know of have lived in Szeged or the surrounding area. Equally important to Lajos is the fact that his mother's family was part of the group of families who held relatively large tracts of land around Szeged prior to the socialist era; they owned more than fifty-seven hectares of land near the Yugoslavian border. In fact, a significant portion of Lajos's life history was taken up with stories of how the family had negotiated with a large Yugoslavian landowner after the Treaty of Trianon to get this land. Part of the Yugoslavian owner's land fell within Hungary's new borders, while part of Lajos' family's land had become part of the new country of Yugoslavia. The two owners traded land for land, and, despite inequalities in quantity and quality, everybody was satisfied.

Lajos also spoke at length of how his parents had moved to Budapest before World War II, yet they had remained tied to the land around Szeged. As I improved my relationship with him and his mother I learned that his mother and her young children had spent much of the war in the capital because her husband had been wounded and was in a hospital on the Pest side of the Danube. Each day she would sneak across one of the bridges to bring him food, sometimes searching for him in the dark when the hospital's electricity supply had been cut. During one of these journeys she was held up on the Buda side of a bridge because of a line of Russian soldiers and as she stood waiting to cross a bomb fell on the bridge, destroying it and all of the people on it.

Eventually, it became very difficult to find food in Budapest and Lajos's mother, along with her father's sister, rode for more than five hours in February on the roof of a train to retrieve provisions from their relatives who had remained on the land near Szeged. Lajos's mother's brother, for whom Lajos is named, was a soldier at the time. Although he had no time to go to the family's land, he also contributed to the survival of his sister's family by trading his cigarette rations for food. Tragically, he disappeared at the end of the war and no one knows what became of him. Before the war ended Lajos's father was dismissed from duty by the Russian army because of an infection and the family returned to the family's land outside of Szeged because, as Lajos said, "During times of instability it is better to live closer to the land." In the early 1950s, all of the family land was lost to collectivization and, by the time Lajos was born, the family was living in Szeged, his mother was working at a variety of places in the city that were willing to overlook her past as a member of the landed class, and his father was drifting into and out of their lives. Although he approached it from many angles, one theme that ties these narratives together is the land and its ability to sustain life, even under the worst circumstances.

Lajos's own connection with his family's land is limited to these stories and to fond memories of the garden house his parents built on a small plot they were able to purchase in the 1970s. He speaks of helping to pick apples and of carrying them to market to sell, as well as helping to weed row after row of peas, carrots, potatoes, and paprika peppers. He is also excited his mother was lucky and was one of the first people to receive compensatory land within the first two years of reprivatization. He believes his mother is renting the land to a cooperative, since she has no use for it herself, but sees it as appropriate that she received compensation in kind for the land that was taken. Like many others, he is disappointed that they weren't able to get back the exact land that had been taken in the 1950s, the land on which his relatives had worked and produced the food that fed his parents, aunts, and uncles.

As for himself, Lajos and his wife spent a couple of difficult years in the 1980s living on a remote farm, or *tanya*, without inside plumbing and gas lines. They lived with an older peasant man, Lajos helping to work the land and care for the animals, Márta caring for the house and cooking for the men. They speak of the work as being very difficult and are incredulous that the peasant man could work so hard and live so simply, but they are also quick to add they enjoyed their time on the land tremendously. When I asked why they moved from the city in which Lajos was born and Márta was educated they said it was romantic to leave society and work the land. Later, Lajos also said he wanted to know the contentment or satisfaction that comes from working on the land. Upon their return to city life they even purchased a garden plot of their own in the hopes that someday they would be able to work the land again and produce food for themselves. Unfortunately, their plot continued to stand empty and unused in 1994 because of the financial strain working it would cause the family. They cannot afford the transportation out to the plot, which is accessible by bus if they had the money to pay almost a dollar each way per person. More importantly, however, Lajos speaks of needing to build a small house on the property before it can be considered usable and they can't afford the transportation, building materials, or the time away from other work. He plans to hold on to the plot, however, because he considers passing a love of the land and the ability to work it on to his children as his ultimate goal. Toward this end he hopes someday he can build a proper garden house and put in a productive garden. For now they only speak of it as a dream for the future.

Irén

Irén was thirty-two, married, and on child-care leave with her almost three-year-old son when I met her in 1993. She, her husband, and their child live in a brand new, three-bedroom apartment in the most expensive and nicest area in Szeged, which she bought after selling a smaller apartment in the city center. Despite the fact that Irén receives less than the equivalent of sixty U.S. dollars per month while on child-care leave and her husband, Attila, makes only an average salary working as a coach and tutor at one of Szeged's technical high schools, this family lives better than most everyone I know in Hungary. They believe their own home, furnishings, clothing, and even their eating habits are comparable to those of western Europeans; and it certainly seemed to be the case. They were the only people I met who had a microwave oven in 1993; they have sophisticated stereo equipment in the family room, the largest refrigerator, two western cars, and only clothing and toys imported from the west. At the same time, both Irén and Attila are very proud of being Hungarian; they teach their son Hungarian legends and folk songs and he can sing these as well as he can sing the theme song from *The Flintstones* (learned from cable television). Both Irén and Attila were tremendously helpful and patient with me, teaching me vocabulary words, grammar structures, idioms, and reviewing my knowledge of Hungarian history, culture, and current events. Without them I could never have accomplished all I did during my seventeen months in Hungary and I have been welcomed back into their home on both of my return trips to Szeged.

Although these friends of mine (the closest thing I made to friends with Hungarians during my time in Szeged) were very mysterious about where the ability to live so well came from, after close to one hundred hours of casual conversations, formal interviews, and a car trip to western Hungary I began to piece things together. Irén and Attila got married only about three years before I met them, when Irén was eight and a half months pregnant. Attila had been married before and has an adult son but this was Irén's first marriage. Prior to this she had spent many years working, both for the state as a translator and privately for a catering service. She had also traveled extensively, visiting places like Egypt, Greece, Japan, Mexico, the United States, and almost every European country. I have no idea how she was able to leave the Eastern bloc more than once every three years, but I did finally learn much of this traveling was paid for by a German boyfriend. In addition, Irén's father is a skilled electrician and has been able to earn well above the national average both before and after his official retirement. When his two children finished school and began living on their own, he gave them each an apartment, furnishings, and anything else they needed to live independently.

Like Lajos's mother, Irén's mother also comes from a family that had acquired a sizable amount of land. She was raised in a village outside of Szeged and, while she was raised on the land and given a regular peasant girl's education, her brother left the village in the mid-1950s to go to college in Budapest. He never returned to live in the village because he was forced to flee the country during the 1956 revolution and now lives in France. Like Lajos's family, Irén's grandparents also lost their land in the 1950s to collectivization and her mother remains thankful she married a man whose life and income are not tied specifically to the land. In the 1970s, however, when Irén was in school, her parents did buy a private home on a large tract, more than a hectare, of productive land. Ever since then both her parents have devoted most of their time during the good weather to growing vegetables. In fact, they produce so much on their plot that, after freezing and canning what they themselves need and giving away as much as their children will take, they compost the rest. They claim it is not worth their time and effort to transport the remainder, which Irén's father estimated to be about half of what they produce, to the market. By the time they factor in the gasoline, their time, and the inevitable waste of produce that spoils before being sold, they would lose money. When I asked why they continue to grow far more than they can use Irén told me her parents were raised that way; her parents told me they enjoy the work, and besides, they own the land so they have to work it.

Unlike Lajos, who derives much of his own identity from his mother's landed past and his own time working and living with a peasant, nothing in Irén's identity comes from a tie to land. She was born and lived the first ten years of her life in a village and her parents continue to grow all their own vegetables, but Irén herself has absolutely no interest in gardening or growing anything. She cites the hard work, the nature of the work, and her satisfaction with the life she has created with her husband and child. She enjoys living in a six-family complex near to the center of town, where she and the other homeowners are able to pay someone to tend the grass and flowers, where she is close to the stores, theaters, and restaurants, and where there are other children with whom her child can play without leaving their backyard. She sees the gardens and the little summer houses located on each small plot as substitutes for what people really want; she feels Hungarians all want something they don't have and settle for these places instead. During the socialist era she thinks Hungarians wanted to travel to the West and to see the world, as she herself was able to do. In the mid-1990s she believed people were afraid and missed the economic security of the past, the kind of security she herself had. Irén describes her position as relatively secure and fulfilled; she has no need for a garden to make her life complete.

Gardens and Security

Examined individually, each of these people seems to have something very different to say about their relationship to the hobby garden. Viki enjoys the ability to work in a way that produces luxury items her family might not buy in the markets, as well as the fresh air and opportunity to get away from the city. She wishes her family had been willing and able to buy more garden plots when they were affordable and also is looking forward to the day when she will be able to put up a building on her own plot, turning it into a real garden. Zoli enjoys the work he is able to do in his gardens, as well as the satisfaction gained by producing far more than his family can use during the year. He believes land must be worked and it would be a tragedy for garden land to sit empty when someone could produce something on it. This sentiment is shared by Zoli, Irén's parents, and countless other Hungarians, even when this means composting or destroying half of what is produced. Lajos has purchased a garden plot because it ties him to the land of his relatives and his own productive past. He cannot spend the time or money now to develop the plot into something useful, even though it would be practical for a vegetarian family of five to grow some of their own food. He and his wife have purchased the plot for their future, when they hope to have the time and money to develop it and put up a small house. Irén has no garden and wants no part of it; in her mind they are a substitute for what people really want and she herself has no need for a substitute for the attainment of a good life.

Despite these different perspectives, all of these people, in addition to many others in Hungary, use the gardens as a way to talk about the kind of secure life they would like to lead, whether this life is a memory from the past, a hope for the future, or positive features of life in the present. Viki and Zoli speak of their gardens as providing access to some of the basic elements of a good life that are absent from their regular, day-to-day existence: fresh air and open space, an abundant supply of luxury items, the promise of productive work. For them, a good life means these elements would be central to their everyday lives and not just to the time spent on their gardens. In Viki's case, the hope for this life rests in the future, when she hopes to marry and combine her small income with her husband's, rather than her mother's retirement benefits, to purchase not only necessities but an occasional luxury item. In Zoli's case, his garden points to his past, when he was able to work and be productive. Lajos's case is a little different from these two. On the one hand, he purchased his garden to recapture a bit of his family's landed past, when his family lived a secure life, as well as his own time spent working the land with a peasant man. On the other hand, his vision of a better life for himself and his wife and children is that they have the time and money to build a garden house and use their land. The unused garden stands as a constant reminder of the time and money he would have if he and his family were more secure. It points both to a comfortable past and the hope for a better future.

Irén exemplifies many of the people I met in Szeged and throughout Hungary who do not own a hobby garden. For them, these gardens are used as a symbol not of some better life, whether this life is in the past or future, but of the secure aspects of their present life. Rather than pointing to some deficiency or want, talk of gardens with people who don't have one often allows them to speak of the good in their present lives. Irén says she does not need a garden because she has achieved her vision of a good life; she travels, lives in a new, comfortable house near to the city, and does not worry about being able to provide the basic necessities for her family. Even poorer people, however, who spend much of their time worried about their job security, salary, or personal situation, point to the things they most cherish, such as children, grandchildren; or a productive past when they say they have no need for a garden. One widow pointed to her apartment, minutes away from a bus line and the shops; her healthy, successful grandchildren; and her utilitarian wardrobe: "I have all I need, why do I need a garden?" Even for these non-owners, the gardens symbolize security. They use them as a way to talk about the positive features of their lives, even if on every other occasion these positive features are overshadowed by poverty, fear, and other aspects of their perceived insecurities. In this time of insecurity, the hobby gardens provide one secure marker against which to measure the crime, unemployment, deprivation, and fear that characterize many people's experience of postsocialist life in Hungary. Even people whose primary form of communication with me was to complain about their insecurity became briefly positive and hopeful when I asked them about gardens or gardening.

While the traditional Hungarian attachment to land and the identification of themselves as workers of the land have taken on new meanings in the postsocialist world, these ideas continue to be used by many to talk about what it means for themselves and others to be Hungarian. When Viki and Lajos speak of needing to erect a small house before their plots can be considered proper gardens, and when Zoli and Irén's father continue to produce fruit and vegetables they have to compost or throw out, it is evident these gardens mean much more to Hungarians than the simple value of the land or the produce. I propose what they mean is membership in the Hungarian nation, that "imagined" community of individuals connected through time, space, and a common agricultural purpose on the land of their ancestors. In other words, it is not only fruit and vegetables that are produced on these gardens but also the nation itself.

According to this conception of the nation, territory must first be turned into land through the addition of both a small house or at the very least a shed, and the planting of domesticated fruit trees, vegetables, and flowers. As one man who has bought, developed, and then sold four different gardens since 1970 says, "I always had to build a house on it." I also saw this in Viki's and Lajos's desire to build houses, or at least sheds, on their plots of garden land before they can be considered real hobby gardens. Second, in order to contribute to the production of the nation, Hungarians must also use every bit of land available for production to its maximum potential. The end result of these actions may be fruit that winds up rotting on the ground below the tree or vegetables that nourish the compost pile rather than human beings, but it is also, in the minds of Hungarians, the nation. This lesson about the importance of using the land was further driven home to me one day when an acquaintance of mine, Tamás, took me to see his ex-wife's garden plot. When they were married, Tamás had built a summer home on the land and planted many trees and a large garden. On the summer day in 1994 when we visited the plot, the garden was covered with dried brush, the trees were unpruned,

The author and Józsi Bacsi, a dear friend and valuable informant.

and it appeared as if nobody had opened the rusty gate in years. Tamás was very sorry the house he had built was sitting empty and falling into disrepair, but what disturbed him most was the waste of potentially productive land. He talked about how in the past he had grown tomatoes, peppers, and cherries. He said, "I made the land useful. Now it's nothing. It's a waste."

While creating gardens and working the land in these ways points to membership in the Hungarian nation, the opposite is also true. In the example above, when Tamás spoke to me of his ex-wife's neglect of the garden he also said she must not be Hungarian to be able to treat a garden this way. Like Tamás, other people also suggested non-Hungarians do not garden. For example, several people claimed Jews and Roma are lazy because they don't work, or at least they don't work the land like a real Hungarian; this sentiment has been noted by other people who have studied Hungary as well (Bell 1984:294). Indeed, until I realized Hungarians do not let anybody else work on their gardens without pay, I wondered if it was my foreignness that made them reluctant to allow me to help.

Clearly, for Tamás, as for so many other Hungarians, gardens represent significant aspects of the imagined Hungarian community. By experiencing agricultural production, even at the very small scale represented by hobby garden production, or by using this kind of production to talk about their lives, individuals connect themselves to what it means to be Hungarian. In part, they imagine themselves as participants in the larger Hungarian national community through their participation in the local community of gardeners. Even when elite members of political and academic circles engage in garden work they do so as "Hungarians" and not as members of these powerful groups. Garden work is the one place in which political, social, and geographic categories break down and individuals act as Hungarians first and foremost.

Conclusion

The complex value system that underlies the institution of the hobby garden in Szeged extends beyond this area of the country. Martha Lampland, an anthropologist who did fieldwork in Hungary during the socialist era, lived in a village far from Szeged. She discovered the reason that the villagers disliked and distrusted the Socialist Workers' Party chairman was not because of his party affiliation but because he did not keep pigs (1991). Like Lampland, I found that privately held gardens and agricultural work were used as symbols by the people of Szeged to discuss what they hold most dear. Unlike her, however, I cannot state definitively that retired people most value the ownership of their own work while younger people most value the imported goods they can buy with garden revenues. What I found instead was that the meaning of the hobby gardens for many Hungarians is a synthesis of both old and new values, of presocialist, socialist, and postsocialist identities. The current concern with security has been mapped on to the traditional view of Hungary as agrarian and modeled on a contemporary idea of peasant values. As a result, in working these gardens and talking about other aspects of their lives in an agrarian idiom, the people of Szeged participate in the construction of the Hungarian nation to the same degree as policy makers and academics do with their productions of national culture. They help imagine the nation into existence and work for its continuation with every moment they spend with their hands in the dirt.

In this chapter I have focused on the ways Hungarians define themselves in a positive mode, in this case as gardeners, while outsiders or Others are those who do not engage in these Hungarian practices or think about their experiences in these terms. In the following chapter I examine some of the ways Hungarian identity is constructed through specific metaphors of difference. On the one hand, I look at the way "balkán" is used as a metaphor in Hungary for all that is negative, and thus non-Hungarian, while on the other hand, other differences are incorporated into a Hungarian identity with relatively little difficulty.

CHAPTER 5

Hungarian Identity in the Context of Otherness

Introduction

The invitation was very inviting: "Come to Istanbul with us!" A U.S.-American friend of mine, Anne, and her Hungarian husband Géza were going to Turkey for a long-awaited vacation and wanted me to come along. They were traveling by bus through Serbia and Bulgaria, which gave me pause but did not immediately deter me. By that time I had been in Hungary for ten months without a break and thought I was due for a vacation. I quickly ran through a list of pros and cons. On the one hand, I would be traveling with a knowledgeable tour guide since Géza spoke and read Turkish and lived in Istanbul as a student. The local representative of the tour company promised that this would be a tourist trip rather than a shopping trip and that we would see two sites outside of Istanbul in addition to the guided tour in the city. I would never again have the opportunity to visit Istanbul for the equivalent of about US$80.00 for hotel and transportation. I would have an entire busload of Hungarians to speak with and get to know—a captive audience for my research questions. In addition, almost every Hungarian I had met had at some time or another taken a bus trip, so, surely, it would have been bad participant observation to have passed up the opportunity to join one of these excursions. On the other hand, traveling through Serbia made me nervous and seventeen hours on a bus seemed extraordinarily long. However, based on the overwhelming number of positives overshadowing these two negatives I decided to go for it. I was headed to Turkey for three and a half days! I gave my deposit money to Géza and it was all settled.

I immediately began telling my other acquaintances about my travel plans, both because I was excited about it and because I knew many of them had been to Istanbul and I wanted their suggestions for sites and restaurants. Their reactions to my news surprised me: "Istanbul?!! What an unsafe trip!" "Why do you want to go to the Balkans?!!" Whereas prior to my announcement I had heard nothing but positive things about Istanbul and Hungarian bus tours generally, afterwards all the responses I heard were overwhelmingly negative. Many people told me all vehicles crossing into Serbia had to grease their entry with goods such as cigarettes, whiskey, and even gold jewelry. Certainly I had heard such tales of bribery before, which was one reason I hadn't traveled outside of Hungary prior to that time. However, the security of the organized tour with a guide and drivers whose very job it was to ease my entry across borders assuaged any nervousness in me that my well-meaning acquaintances tried to stir up. Indeed, the up-front cost of the trip included a fifteen-German-mark surcharge per person for bribe money! Surely that would cover any difficulties we encountered along the way (West 2000).

Even with this assurance, Hungarians insisted crossing into Serbia would not be as easy as promised. One person told me Hungarian buses were often forced by Serbian border guards to unpack all of their bags and goods purchased in Istanbul, pack them into a truck, and then pay enormous fees to ship the load across the country. The guards claim these buses are passenger and not shipping vehicles and thus they are required to provide trucks and drivers for the goods, at great cost to everyone on the bus. I was relatively unconcerned by this information as well, since the tour guide with whom Géza had dealt had promised this would be a tourist trip and not one designed for "shoppers." I use this term as comparable to Konstantinov's "trader-tourists" (1996:762). For Hungarians, this practice in the mid-1990s entailed travel to Istanbul, Turkey; Trieste, Italy; Graz, Austria, or any other destination primarily to buy large amounts of clothing, jewelry, and other goods for resale in Hungary, whether legally or not.

Other stories of border misadventures, however, were less easily dismissed as irrelevant to my impending journey. One particular story, repeated by a number of people independently of each other, was especially disturbing. I was told one Hungarian bus had been pulled over in Serbia and a border guard had raped a young woman before allowing the bus to proceed (see West 1997, 2000). No one was able to provide the specifics, such as names, dates, newspaper citations, or the like, but all believed not only in the possibility of such an event occurring but that it had indeed happened. Despite myself, the image of a heavily armed guard raping an innocent woman flitted in and out of my mind whenever I thought about my upcoming adventure. I took slim comfort in the belief that if this tale was true, and it happened again, the guard probably would not choose Anne or me. Neither of us conformed very well to Serbian (or Hungarian, for that matter) ideas about women's clothes, hair, make-up, and other local symbols of femininity, at least from what I had seen of Serbians who came to Szeged to shop.

As it turned out, this trip and one other bus journey, to Paris, Strasbourg, and the Loire Valley, were two of the best fieldwork tools I employed during my months in Hungary. The trip reinforced the idea that contrast is the essence of vision (Benz 1996). Many aspects of Hungarian identity that are self-evident for Hungarians when they are at home, and thus are not easily drawn into conversation, are brought into the open as soon as they leave their comfortable surroundings. Much as anthropologists are forced to think about aspects of their own cultures and identities during fieldwork, these Hungarians were much better able to speak about their identity in the face of cultural difference than while sitting in their own living rooms. At the same time, these trips also helped me to understand the ways Hungarians understand and ascribe meaning to different kinds of foreigners.

These trips were certainly not the first experiences I had in which I learned about Hungarian attitudes toward foreigners. I had often felt uncomfortable in conversations with acquaintances about these attitudes; many expressed greater or lesser degrees of dislike and distrust. Crime, pollution, even unemployment were often blamed on foreign visitors or foreign residents of Szeged. These were fairly common conversation topics with people of all backgrounds, despite the fact that, clearly, I was a foreigner in Hungary. I did not understand how they could be saying something so negative about me, directly to me. Yet I did not ask them about their beliefs, either because I did not want to know their response or because I was able to convince myself that they thought differently about me because I spoke their language and lived in Szeged. I now realize they were able to have these conversations with me, to complain to their foreign acquaintance about the problems caused by foreigners, because despite my foreignness I was not the Other. I was an Other, clearly, but not the particular Other through which Hungarian identity was most clearly articulated at that time (West 2000). The referent in these discourses about the problems caused by foreigners is not foreigners in general but a particular set of foreigners, the residents of countries *believed by Hungarians* to be Balkan, especially Serbia, Romania, Bulgaria, Turkey, and Ukraine (see Todorova 1997).

In this chapter I tell the story of this trip to Istanbul and follow it with discussions on several issues raised by my descriptions. These issues concern not only Hungarian identity constructions that define the Hungarian self in relation to other, imagined identities (Balkan, European), but also other aspects of Hungarian identity that were made clearer to me during the two bus trips and my whole fieldwork period in general. I have written myself into this chapter in a very self-conscious way in order to show how some aspects of Hungarian identity conflict with my own ideas about the world and my place in it. The result is often comparative; however, these comparisons are not made in order to judge or evaluate, but rather to explain some of the ways I came to understand a Hungarian worldview and the place of the individual in it. Certainly a different anthropologist would have had different experiences, made different comparisons, and felt differently about his or her own confrontations with otherness; however, these differences would be less about Hungarian identities than those of the anthropologists.

The Journey

My trip to Istanbul began around 11:00 A.M. on the last Sunday of October, 1993. I braced myself against a cold wind and walked into town to catch the bus, which was supposed to pick us up in front of Szeged's city hall at 11:30. When I arrived, Anne and Géza were huddled together on a bench, while a number of other people, presumably fellow tourists, were standing next to a couple of cars. At 11:45, Géza had a quick conversation with the others to find that only one couple would be accompanying us; the other people were their children and parents who had come to see them off. This couple had also been told the bus would leave at 11:30, so we weren't alone in our apprehension that somehow the bus had missed its Szeged stop. While the three of us jumped around to keep warm, took turns walking up the block to look for the bus, and tried to contact the tour company representative by phone, our fellow travelers and their entourage climbed back into their cars to wait, protected somewhat from the bitter wind.

In all, we waited for close to six hours that afternoon, although not all of it outside and not all of it in complete ignorance of the situation at hand. At 1:30, after we'd been outside for more than two hours, eaten our picnic lunch, and purchased chocolate bars and cans of Coke at the only shop in the city center open that day, a waiter from a nearby restaurant came out to speak with us. He asked if we were waiting for a tour bus to Istanbul. Surprised, but relieved someone knew we were there waiting, we said yes. Unfortunately, he did not have good news. The restaurant had received a phone call from

Traffic waiting to enter Hungary from Yugoslavia, November 1993.

Budapest; the bus had experienced brake problems, had been forced to turn around to be repaired in the capital, and would arrive three hours later. He was unclear if that meant three hours from the estimated time of arrival at 11:30 or three hours from the present time.

We were both upset at the news and glad to be given a reprieve from our outside vigil. We discussed the option of going home for a short while, but, because of the uncertainty over when the three-hour period began, decided we'd better not. Instead, we gathered up our bags and went into the restaurant for a second lunch of hot soup, tea, and coffee. Even that relief was short lived, however, since, being a Sunday afternoon, the restaurant shut its doors at 4:00 and asked the three lone customers to leave. We spent the last hour and a half outside, jumping up each time we heard a city bus, tram, taxi, or private automobile approaching the square. By the time the bus arrived at 5:30, the last gray fingers of light were fading, we were bitterly cold, and nothing could have stopped us from finally boarding the long-awaited bus.

At first, however, we did waver uncertainly about joining this group. The passengers who had boarded in Budapest warned us, in a half-hearted way, about the possible dangers and added expense of traveling into Serbia. We began to think more seriously about the warnings we had received from others prior to that day. The bus's mechanical problems also seemed like a good reason for abandoning the plan. However, in the end, no tale of possible corruption or delay sounded worse than having to walk home in the cold after an entire day wasted, waiting for a trip that didn't happen. We very much wanted to go to Istanbul. The tour guide who was to accompany the trip also seemed very candid and honest and then, somehow, the representative who had sold the trip to my friends (whom we had been unable to reach by telephone) appeared just at that moment to provide more reassurance. The two tour company employees assured us that the only problem might occur as we crossed into Serbia a mere fifteen kilometers from Szeged and suggested if at that point we felt threatened, the bus would bring us back and refund our deposit. It seemed as if we had nothing to lose by joining the group. Our luggage was stowed underneath the bus and we took three seats near the driver.

Leaving Hungary was very easy. The guard stamped my passport without even pausing to read my entry stamp, an illegible spot of ink given to me months earlier on the Austrian-Hungarian border. Gaining entry into Serbia, however, was not quite so simple. As the well-armed guard moved toward us from the back of the bus, stamping Hungarian passports as he went, I began to get nervous. After many long hours of being detained at an international border crossing years before, no matter how friendly the country is to U.S.-American tourists or how indisputable my papers, I always have this reaction at border crossings. And, as was apparent from this Serbian guard's array of weapons and everyone's nervous quiet as he passed by, this was not like any other crossing I had endured up to this point.

When the guard got to Anne's and my passports you could almost see the gleam in his eyes; he collected them from both of us, grunted "*viza, viza,*" and got off the bus. The information we had gotten from the travel agent and the Yugoslavian consulate in Hungary was that U.S.-Americans were not required to obtain a visa for transit across Serbia. However, it would seem no one had told this particular guard about the regulations; our protests that we were not required to purchase a visa were ignored as he exited with our passports. Minutes later, five or thirty-five I don't know since adrenaline and the stress of the entire day had disoriented my sense of time, the bus driver came back to say we were each being charged fifteen German marks plus two cartons of cigarettes for our transit visas. "What transit visas?" we asked; "U.S.-Americans do not need transit visas!" Unfortunately, this fact was clearly irrelevant to the situation at hand. Either we paid the money, got our passports back, and completed our trip or we refused and, well, nobody knew what would happen then. We conferred. I thought about the raped woman with a little less incredulity than I had just hours before. Was the trip worth this? Did we want to turn around and go back to Szeged? The tour company representative tried to reassure us this would be the only trouble we would have since it was a transit visa good for seven days. But, before we had made up our minds, the driver returned with our stamped passports to collect our money. Every choice but to pay him and continue traveling had been taken away from us. We were going through Serbia, and supporting someone's nicotine habit at the same time. We complained but each gave the driver fifteen marks and the money to purchase cigarettes from the bus's stash of bribery goods. It seemed unfair that, essentially, we had had to purchase those same cigarettes twice, the first time with the mandatory fifteen-mark fee we paid when we booked the trip and then this second time, but the driver didn't see things our way so we were out of luck. Not long afterwards, sleep came as a welcome respite from the injustice we felt had been heaped upon us that day.

Unfortunately, our respite did not last long. Every forty-five minutes or so, an armed military patrol unit stopped the bus and demanded goods from the driver before allowing us to pass. At one of these stops we watched as the driver heaped eight cartons of cigarettes onto the outstretched hands of the guard before he allowed us to pass. At another of these stops Géza, who also understands some Serbo-Croatian, heard the guards arguing with the patrolman: "We don't have coffee! We have gold, leather, whiskey, sugar, but no coffee!" I do not know what he finally settled for. Another patrolman requested two aspirin and a hot cup of tea before allowing us to pass by his section of highway. Many of the women passengers dug into their purses to find the necessary aspirin so we could continue. It was unbelievable! Here we were, riding along on the best maintained, most well-lit stretch of highway I had seen since leaving western Europe almost a year earlier, while the people who were expected to maintain order on them were demanding goods for the black market. I was disconcerted by their ability to run such a renegade bureaucracy in Europe in 1993, as well as by the obvious shortages and difficulties causing them to resort to this method of supplementing their wages.

These short delays were just the prelude to the much longer stop we experienced at around 2:30 A.M. We had been moving along fairly steadily, not having been stopped for quite awhile, when all of a sudden we pulled off to the side of the road. There were no lights, no buildings, no apparent reason for our stop, and the drivers would not allow us to get off the bus so we remained seated, wondering to ourselves what could be wrong now. The bus remained motionless for more than an hour and, although we were prevented from disembarking, one driver and then another got off and on the bus several times while all the passengers slept or tried to in the cold bus. Eventually, I smelled gasoline and figured we had just stopped to refuel. I couldn't imagine why we had sat for so long before being allowed to purchase the fuel, or why the station had no lights, but just assumed it had something to do with the shortages in Serbia. It turned out, however, our drivers had arranged before the trip to meet some Serbian acquaintances or business partners in order to sell them fuel the U.N. embargo was preventing them from getting at reasonable prices at home. On account of the mechanical problems and subsequent late start, the contacts had gone home and we had had to wait for them to arrive after our drivers called them. So, not only were we left sitting in the cold for over an hour but we were also running the U.N. embargo! Later in the trip I spoke with a few of the other passengers about this fuel incident, people who made this trip on a monthly basis, and they said this was a fairly regular occurrence. On the return trip our drivers did the same thing, this time in the light of day. We considered taking photographs of the sale but did not want to risk losing our cameras and photographs of Istanbul to an angry Hungarian bus driver or Serb "businessman."

Just before dawn we finally crossed out of Serbia and into Bulgaria. This border crossing was uneventful, although the drivers did have to buy our way into the country with cartons of cigarettes and bottles of whiskey from the bus's stash of goods. Despite the ease with which these transactions were done, I was very nervous due to our previous experience with borders and very glad when we pulled over for a break just over the border. This time we sat in a deserted gas station for more than twenty minutes while the drivers discussed the sensibility of continuing forward with mere fumes in the fuel tank. Thankfully, they decided to wait for the station to open. This gave us the opportunity to watch the sunrise over the frozen, desolate Bulgarian landscape, the sun providing backlighting for a factory spewing smoke and flame several miles to the east of us. More importantly, it gave me time to explore the area for an open restroom. I looked around and by following my nose found a closed door behind the station. I was in luck! By this time many of the other women had followed my exit from the bus, but, much to my surprise, they elected to squat in the bushes rather than use the toilet. They said I should follow their lead because it would be a "balkán" toilet, which they pronounced with such scorn that I had to stick my head in the door, if just to see what they meant. It turned out to be what I knew as a Turkish or squat toilet: a hole in the floor with foot pads, to facilitate squatting over the hole.

In weighing my options I decided getting out of the cold wind was preferable to avoiding the so-called "balkán" toilet, particularly since I was essentially squatting on the ground in either case.

Fortunately, after our brief stop, the trip through Bulgaria was as uneventful as it was interesting. While Serbia had made Hungary's infrastructure seem old and decrepit in comparison, Bulgaria's in contrast made Hungary seem wealthy and modern. We saw no more than a dozen other motorized vehicles on the road in Bulgaria and few signs the road had been repaired or updated in years. Later that day, our immediate impression of Turkey was equally interesting; it was like stepping back into the Western world. We were greeted by huge, brightly colored billboards of the sort that line many U.S.-American highways, Shell and Mobil petrol stations, and, at the border crossing itself, an unarmed guard who sat in front of computer terminals and barely noticed our U.S.-American passports as he stamped them desultorily.

Despite all of the difficulties, disappointments, and hidden costs of this trip, we had a wonderful time in Istanbul. On our first evening, Anne, Géza, and I had dinner in a restaurant whose large windows faced the beautiful Blue Mosque and as we dined the meuzzin called the faithful to prayer with his, to my ears, haunting cries. One afternoon we joined a few other curious members of our group for a tour of Istanbul that included a ferry ride across the Bosporus to the Asian half of the city. For lunch that day we ate the freshest fish I've ever purchased. It was caught off one side of a wildly rocking twelve-foot boat as we watched, cleaned and cooked on the boat, and then sold off the other side to eager Turkish businessmen, students, and, on that day, two U.S.-American and a Hungarian tourist. We explored many miles of the tunnels and passageways that constitute the famous Grand Bazaar, filled with carpets, pottery, clothing, and other items. We also visited the Egyptian Bazaar, where small animals and birds, spices, tea, and other food items are sold, mostly to the local population. We tried our hand at haggling, purchased a half dozen Turkish tiles, and were swindled by the seller of a beautiful little vase, which somehow got wrapped and pushed into our hands before we could observe its very noticeable flaws.

We spoke with young boys who were hawking socks, purses, perfumes, and various other small items from their plastic bag warehouses and older, more experienced salesmen who sold from tables set up on the sidewalk or adjacent to the many bazaars. Each time we were amazed at the knowledge these boys and men had of foreign currencies and languages. It is possible in the area of Istanbul where we stayed to use almost any currency anywhere, whether it is a department store or street seller; even the non-convertible Hungarian forint was welcomed everywhere I tried to use it. The same can be said with regard to languages; I spoke with one young man who spoke English quite well and challenged me to find a language in which he could not greet the customer and haggle over prices. I do not know the degree to which he made up his greetings in Estonian and Swahili, but in the languages with which my friends and I were acquainted he was always able to make his point understood: English, Hungarian, French, Spanish, German, Russian, Serbo-Croatian, and, obviously, Turkish. It was a fascinating experience to be in Istanbul even for just three days.

Indeed, as it turned out we were in the city for longer than we had expected. We were supposed to have breakfast on Thursday morning, have a couple hours in the morning to do last-minute shopping or sightseeing, and then meet the group back in the hotel lobby around 11:00 to pack the bus and get on the road. Needless to say, things did not turn out that way. The bus that had brought us to Istanbul on Monday did not stay in the city while we shopped and toured. It went back to Hungary with a group it had dropped off in Turkey several days before, and would be bringing another group on the day we were supposed to begin our trip back. However, the brake problem that had delayed the beginning of our journey by half a day had destroyed any schedule the bus may have maintained at one time. We did not leave Istanbul until just after 3:00 P.M.

Unfortunately, our hopes for a more pleasant trip home than the journey there did not last very long. As we pulled out of the city the guide announced our late start would prevent us from stopping to see the mosque at Edirne. We had been promised two visits to sites outside of Istanbul, Rákóczi's house, where the eighteenth-century Hungarian revolutionary leader resided after the Hungarian defeat at the hands of the Habsburgs, and the mosque at Edirne. The first of these sites was closed on Mondays and, as this trip always arrives in Turkey on Mondays, is never shown, while the second could have been visited as we entered Turkey but was passed up for a forty-five minute break at a rest stop along the highway, not more than ten miles from Edirne. We became very angry at the tour company for lying to us, the guide and drivers for not stopping at the mosque previously, and the Hungarians on the bus who were completely unconcerned with any of these issues.

We became even more riled when, just after passing out of Turkey, we stopped in what seemed like the middle of nowhere, Bulgaria, for cheese. It was very clear, regardless of the saleswoman's pitch, not only was this trip accommodating to Hungarian shoppers, it was designed specifically for them. The women who were sitting across the bus's aisle from us were regulars on this Budapest-Istanbul route and shopped for several boutiques in the capital. Each boutique owner either gave them a specific list of items he or she wanted them to purchase in the Turkish bazaars or gave them suggestions for things the shop might be able to resell quickly. A woman who had taken two sleeping pills and then stretched out in a sleeping bag on the bus's floor next to us on the trip there was also shopping for resale in Hungary. Rather than serving as go-betweens, she and her husband sold the items themselves in various outdoor markets in the Budapest area. After a bit of investigating, we learned that Anne, Géza, the other couple from Szeged, one woman from Budapest, and I were the only tourists on the bus. In fact, the guide herself had once been a shopper and had been hired by the company specifically to make the way for other shoppers easier! This fact became more and more obvious throughout the trip: when our complaints about missing the trips outside of Istanbul were brushed aside, when the guide tried to lead a tour around Istanbul and had to read all of the information from a book, and when we saw the enormous amount of baggage our fellow travelers were bringing back to Hungary. The agency's promise that this was a tourist trip was entirely fabricated. As we had done on the trip there, we tried to use sleep to get away from our emotions. It was dark in Bulgaria anyway so our chances of enjoying the countryside were slim.

Things went very smoothly again on the route through Bulgaria but as we approached the Serbian border I was nauseous with nerves, as was Anne. We tried to convince ourselves that we had already purchased transit visas so we had nothing to worry about, but in light of the brigandage we had witnessed on the way through Serbia the first time, this was of little comfort. As it turned out, we were correct in our assumption that the tour guide didn't know what she was talking about when she assured us there would be no problem at this end. The Serbian guard who stamped the Hungarian passports without batting an eye collected the two U.S.-American passports and exited the bus with them. We were subjected to another tense wait, charged another ten German marks each, and issued another unnecessary visa. We sighed with relief, however, upon receiving our passports back and congratulated each other that the visa at this end did not include cartons of cigarettes.

Our celebration, however, was ephemeral. About a hundred yards beyond the passport control section of the Bulgarian-Serbian border there is a manually controlled gate to allow cars, trucks, and buses into the country. We were extremely anxious and at this point even the Hungarians on the bus began to get a little nervous. It was at this point, they told us, that they might have to unload all their goods and pack them into a truck, for which they would have to pay dearly to get their purchases across Serbia. My stomach flip-flopped as the bus was pulled over and an armed guard entered and began checking passports. He was not very careful about it and was merely looking at their covers. Maybe, I thought, I could get away with him not noticing me, since both U.S.-American and Hungarian passports are blue. He walked slowly toward our section of the bus and then passed me by without carefully examining the blue booklet I held upside down, to conceal the gold lettering that boldly declared: Passport, United States of America. Unfortunately, Anne was not as disingenuous as I was and had her passport taken away from her. I felt badly that Anne was having to suffer alone for a crime of which we were both guilty, being U.S.-American in a country suffering from international sanctions supported by our government, but at the same time I was relieved I had been spared. My ambivalence did not last long, however, for after speaking with the guard, the bus driver announced that because the bus was Hungarian any non-Hungarian citizen wanting to travel on it through Serbia would be charged one hundred German marks. The guard had also inspected the bus's passenger list and, even though he had not taken my passport, he knew the bus contained two U.S.-Americans and two Romanians in addition to its Hungarian passengers.

Instead of charging for the truck, which would not produce much of a profit margin for the guards, they had decided (perhaps at the request of the driver) to invent a rule about foreign passengers. Rather than Hungarian shoppers who, by their own calculations, were poised to make tens of thousands of forints from this trip, it was the relatively poor U.S.-American graduate student and language teacher who were being charged one hundred marks each. Admittedly, Anne and I come from a much wealthier country than Hungary, but at that time we were each earning significantly less per month than any of these shoppers made in a week. We tried arguing with the guide that we were not personally responsible for these fees but the bus was; the company had agreed to transport us regardless of our citizenship and it was therefore up to the company to get us home again. She said this was not the case; the bribe fund to which we had all contributed was not large enough and the passengers had already had to contribute to a fund to reimburse one of the drivers for his gold watch after a Bulgarian guard demanded it. We next argued that all the passengers would have had to pitch in for the truck if it had been required so why shouldn't everyone be required to pitch in for this. Again, the gold watch was cited and we were assured this was our problem.

We were on our own. Either the bus left us there on the frozen Bulgarian-Serbian border at 3:30 A.M., with very little money and no way to get to Sofia to fly back to Hungary, or we had to come up with the marks. I wanted to test their resolve, to refuse to pay or to get off the bus, but Anne and Géza had already decided we had been sitting at the border long enough and it would be better just to pay her fee in order to get moving again. I could not sit back and allow my friends to empty their wallets alone so I handed over the last dollars and marks I had with me as well. They did not add up to one hundred marks so I borrowed most of the difference from my friends, and watched as a collection taken up by one of the passengers heavily subsidized the Hungarian-Romanian shoppers' entry into Serbia. Once the bus was moving again, all the stress of the encounter exploded out of Anne and me in bouts of hysterical laughter and crying combined. By borrowing money I had just spent my food budget for the entire month and was going to have to find new students to tutor in English if I wanted to eat. Anne had wiped out her Christmas fund and wasn't sure how she was going to purchase gifts or cards that year. At first, a few of the other passengers tried to comfort us but, since in our state neither of us could speak much Hungarian, they eventually left us alone to work through our obviously traumatic experience. In the end, we decided that although we were angry and tired and anxious, the fact that we were also completely out of money was almost a relief. No one could ask us to finance any more bribes; we simply had nothing more to contribute.

As with our first journey across Serbia, on the return trip the bus was again stopped every hour or so. Even during the light of day armed guards openly stopped vehicles at will and demanded cigarettes, whiskey, clothing, or most anything they desired. Once again we stopped at a designated spot and siphoned off two barrels of fuel into the containers of a waiting group of

Serbian men. Once again we were very impressed by the high quality and good maintenance of Serbia's infrastructure in comparison with Hungary's. And once again we got very nervous as we approached the border. However, this time we were not alone in our nervousness. The Hungarian shoppers were getting anxious about bringing such large amounts of foreign goods into Hungary. Hungarians must pay a forty-five percent customs tax on every item they bring back into the country, which severely cuts into profits for both go-betweens and independent sellers alike. We were asked by numerous people, the same people who refused to help us at the other Serbian border, if we would carry a piece of luggage for them, or wear a leather jacket or gold ring. As foreigners we were not required to pay anything. We told them we would think about it, but in light of their lack of willingness to help us we knew we would never cooperate.

It was close to noon by the time we reached the stationary line of trucks, buses, and passenger vehicles that indicated the Hungarian border was only a few hundred yards away. We ate the last of the bread and fruit we had purchased in Istanbul, got off the bus to stretch our legs a bit, and spoke with other Hungarian groups waiting for the line to move. We learned some of them had been waiting for as long as five or six hours just to reach this point in the line. We also learned a shopping bus somewhere ahead of us in line contained a dead body. According to the story passing from bus to bus, a group of shoppers had stopped at the Topkapi Palace in Istanbul on their way home. While they were inside the palace, presumably Turkish thieves had cleaned out the bus of all the clothes, jewelry, and other items they had purchased with the intention of reselling in Hungary. One of the passengers had taken it so badly, it was said, she had a heart attack. She complained to the people around her she didn't feel well and they recommended sleep. After several hours someone realized she was no longer sleeping but dead. We never heard any more details of the supposed heart attack; indeed, after our return I checked into the story in local and national newspapers and could find no reference to it whatsoever. As with the story of the Serbian guard and the rape of a Hungarian woman, to this day I do not know if this really happened or if it was just a myth of Hungarian victimization at the hands of foreign criminals.

Finally, after nearly three hours, we had had enough standing around in a line that was not moving anywhere. We were frustrated and angry at having our time wasted; we were also nervous that by staying with the shopping bus we were somehow going to wind up further in debt just to exit Serbia or enter Hungary. So, along with Anne, Géza, the other couple from Szeged, and the one tourist from Budapest, I picked up my relatively tiny piece of luggage in order to walk the last few hundred yards to the border. At this point even one of the drivers agreed this was a good idea for us. However, a few passengers who seemed to think we had agreed to carry their oversized luggage over the border for them were very disappointed and even angry at our decision to leave them. One passenger was particularly pushy about it; as I got off the bus to begin walking she handed me a leather jacket, as if she needed me to hold it while she tied her shoe or straightened her bag. Instead, she began with a long explanation about how she would have to pay an import tax of forty-five percent on the jacket but because I'm not Hungarian I would be able to bring it in for nothing. I laughed and tossed the jacket back at her. When we were in trouble at the Bulgarian-Serbian border neither this woman nor her traveling companions contributed to our one-hundred-mark fees. Regardless of her protests now there was no way I was going to give her a hand. In fact, her audacity continued to cause ripples of laughter in our little band of tourists as we hiked to the border.

As it turns out, leaving the bus was probably the best decision we made on the entire trip. We were allowed through Serbian immigration without a single problem, although we had removed our rings, earrings, and watches just in case. Speaking with the Hungarian guard on the other side was one of the most joyous moments of my whole fieldwork experience. The young soldier laughed at our tale of unnecessary visas and exorbitant fees and said, as he stamped us into Hungary, "Yes, that's the way the Serbs are: 'balkán.'" I had never been so thrilled to be in Hungary as I was for the first few minutes after receiving that stamp. We were home; we were safe. The local Szeged bus arrived within the next half hour and, hoping no inspector would be on it since we had no tickets or money to purchase them, we boarded and headed for Anne and Géza's stop. Fortunately, our luck held and we arrived back in Szeged without being asked to show our tickets. After a brief meeting in their living room to determine when we could go to complain to the travel agent who had booked the tour, my friends drove me home. The journey was finally over.

Balkán

Although it should be quite obvious by now what Hungarians mean when they use "balkán" as an adjective and an epithet, I explicate it here because of the frequency with which I encountered the term during my fieldwork (see West 2000). Geographically and historically, the term Balkan refers to the countries of the Balkan Peninsula: Albania, Bulgaria, Greece, Romania, Turkey, and the republics, enclaves, and zones that made up Yugoslavia between 1920 and 1990. The term also names the mountain range that runs through what was formerly eastern Yugoslavia and Bulgaria to the Black Sea, and is used in reference to the wars waged in this area of Europe in 1912 and 1913. However, when Hungarians use the term they are generally not referring specifically to any of these geographic features or historic events. "Balkán" in Hungarian is more of a metaphor that connotes a whole host of characteristics and features Hungarians see as diametrically opposed to themselves; I indicate their usage of the term by spelling it in Hungarian and putting it in quotation marks: "balkán." To be "balkán" is to be dirty, violent, dismissive of rules and laws, even uncivilized. To be sure, some Hungarians would attribute these traits to some of the peoples of the

Balkans. For example, the wars and fighting plaguing the former Yugoslavia were pointed to repeatedly to illustrate characteristic "balkán" behavior (see West 2000; Todorova 1997). However, this characterization is in way no limited to this region, and, conversely, some of the peoples and places of the Balkans proper would not be characterized by most Hungarians as "balkán," e.g., Greeks.

The bus trip to Istanbul allowed me to see many of the ways this opposition between Hungarian and "balkán" was constructed and subsequently experienced. However, even before this trip the reactions I received from acquaintances about what it would be like revealed quite a bit about how Hungarians see themselves in relation to those assumed to be "balkán." Adjectives like dirty, dangerous, and cheap were used to speak of Istanbul. Likewise, our path through Serbia was seen as fraught with danger because of its quintessential "balkán" character. Nonetheless, our choice to go across Serbia instead of Romania was praised, since Romania is seen as even more dangerous, more of an outlaw state, or even just more "balkán," than any of the chaotic, internationally sanctioned regions of the former Yugoslavia. Indeed, when the non-Hungarians on the bus faced the one-hundred-mark fee per person at the Bulgarian-Serbian border, we asked if it would be possible to take an alternative route back through Romania. We were told in no uncertain terms that a route through Romania would be more difficult for a Hungarian bus than one through Serbia. Perhaps because of their long history of disagreement over Transylvania, with both countries claiming national historical precedence and territorial legitimacy in the area, and the ongoing disagreement between the two states over the treatment of Hungarian minorities in Romania, the Romanian people are believed to be even more vicious toward Hungarians than southern Slavs. While both populations are characterized as "balkán," with all the term connotes in Hungarian, Romanians are seen as malicious toward Hungarians specifically while southern Slavs are seen as merely uncivilized generally. The two Hungarian-Romanian shoppers on the bus readily confirmed this sentiment as well. Therefore, most people were uncertain whether we, as U.S.-Americans, would fare any better going through Romania than Serbia, but all were positive a Hungarian bus would have great difficulty passing through Romania without being stripped of all valuable property. In both cases, the opposition of these countries' people and characteristics to Hungary, Hungarians, and Hungarianness is explicable for Hungarians with just one word: "balkán."

Clues to the intellectual and emotional contents of this opposition in the 1990s were given to me at other times throughout this trip as well. In response to my question of why Hungarian border guards do not require goods or money before allowing people to enter their country, most people said it was because Hungary is civilized, like Europe, whereas its neighbors are "balkán." One woman did say a few Hungarian guards are becoming greedy and demanding leather jackets or gold but she also said this was the fault of foreigners, clearly "balkán" foreigners, who come to Hungary and expect to have to treat officials this way. The Hungarian guards do not refuse when offered such gifts to speed along the entry of these foreigners and a few guards have even come to expect such "gifts." Everyone who heard the woman telling me this story agreed that it is a shame that a few Hungarians have become "balkán." At my suggestion that their own desire and machinations to cheat the Hungarian government out of its forty-five percent customs duty on their goods were comparable to the behavior of these guards or that of the Serbian guards, I was immediately told that this was not so. In fact, they argued, it is the Hungarian government that is being "balkán" in this case, robbing them of the profits of their hard work, and they are just trying to survive in these difficult and insecure times (see West 2000).

Another incident that illustrates the oppositional use of "balkán" in the construction of Hungarian identity occurred just after we crossed into Serbia on our return trip. One woman, who praised me often on my ability to speak Hungarian, went on to say that during this bus trip I had become more Hungarian. Because I had experienced the "balkán" character, its dishonesty and meanness, I must now understand why the Hungarians hate and distrust the southern Slavs, especially Serbs, to the degree they do. For a brief moment I was proud of the fact that I had become more Hungarian on this trip and that Hungarians were beginning to think of me as one of them. However, the more I thought about the context of the compliment, the more I realized the danger of ethnocentrism in the fieldwork setting. Not only must fieldworkers try not to judge others based on the norms and values of their own societies, but they must also be careful not to take on the ethnocentric and even racist attitudes of their host societies. Although it is impossible for anyone, anthropologists included, to attain objectivity or to remain neutral, the anthropologist's job is to describe and analyze cultural difference, not outwardly judge it.

Through my experiences in Szeged and on these trips I eventually learned that all that is Hungarian is, ideally, the opposite of "balkán;" it is clean, honorable, European, civilized. I heard quite often that one of the most serious problems affecting Hungary and Hungarians in the postsocialist era is the influx of "balkán" ideas, values, and even people. I spoke with most everyone I met about what Szeged and Hungary were like in 1993–94 in comparison with five, ten, twenty, fifty years earlier. Although I am positive a certain amount of nostalgia for some idealized past colors all of their descriptions, I cannot dismiss the fact so many Hungarians blamed the dirt, crime, disorder, and every other negative change they feel Szeged and Hungary have experienced, in a word, the insecurity, on "balkán" influences. There is no denying that in Szeged, at this time, the particular Other against which the nation was defined was the "balkán" Other.

I have to conclude this section with a reminder that "balkán," when used in this way, is largely a metaphor with only a partial connection to the geographic region bearing the same name. This point was made to me when the Hungarian government was referred to as "balkán" for demanding large customs duty on imported goods, and when the Hungarian guards who have begun to demand goods were labeled as such. Similarly, when Romanians were described as "more 'balkán'" than Serbs it was obvious the term had little to do with geography or history, and almost everything to do with Hungarian ideas about themselves and others. A Hungarian acquaintance of mine from Budapest who was living in London in 1998 told me that even parts of southeast Hungary are more "balkán" than European (West 2000:58), which, of course, would anger people from Szeged very much. When I asked her to explain what she meant, she said the region was less developed, the people more backward, and the whole area just different from the rest of Hungary. Finally, when I heard a public restroom in Germany described by Hungarians as "balkán" I knew I was dealing with something other than hatred of the neighbors or "internal orientalism" (West 2000, n.55). This event happened during my second bus trip, from Szeged to France, when we stopped at a highway rest stop. I entered the women's restroom to find the Hungarian women all waiting in line, despite the fact that two stalls remained empty. When I asked if the toilets were out of order, I was told instead that they were "balkán." I was a little unsure about what the women meant because of the variety of connotations the term carries in Hungarian; however, from my previous experience I was fairly certain these toilets were broken, disgustingly dirty, or simply squat toilets. I looked around the restroom briefly, saw it was pristine, and took my chances that these were squat toilets and not broken or disgusting toilet bowls. I was correct.

Europe

While "balkán" is a metaphor used by many people in Szeged to describe Hungary and Hungarians oppositionally, Europe has a much more ambivalent meaning. The idea that Hungarians are an Eastern people who settled in Europe, or the West, in 896 C.E., is one that has guided poetry, politics, and even ethnography in that country for many centuries (West 2000:55–7). In some contexts, such as in the nineteenth century when Hungarian nationalists were trying to separate their country from Habsburg domination, Hungary's Eastern origins were highlighted to depict differences from Austrians. In other contexts, such as the postsocialist governments' moves towards alliance with and membership in NATO and the EU, a European identity is embraced. In both cases, as well as numerous others (see chapter 2), the idea of Europe cannot be seen as unequivocally bad or good. While both Europe and the West are developed, modern, civilized, and efficient, they are also superficial, lacking in community, greedy, and impersonal.

Despite this historic ambivalence with the idea, my own experience in Hungary was that Europe was used primarily as a positive referent. Prior to my leaving for Istanbul, I was told over and over again I should stay in Europe and go to Italy or Austria if I wanted to do some shopping, as most people assumed I was doing in Istanbul, rather than risking my neck in the

Balkans. Numerous Hungarians also used "European" as a descriptive term meaning high quality. For example, the goods available in these other popular shopping destinations were said to be of much higher quality than those from Turkey. Similarly, when discussing a pair of sandals I had purchased at a local shoe store, one of my acquaintances told me they were cheap and poorly made, not like her own "European" ones, which, to me, looked almost identical, right down to their "Made in China" label.

In addition to signifying safety and quality, Europe for many Hungarians also signifies aspects of their own identities they feel were denied to them during the socialist era. For example, when I spoke with my traveling companions on the bus to France about why they had chosen that trip, many told me it was an opportunity to explore aspects of their common tradition as Europeans that had been denied to them by the Soviets and their "foreign," meaning non-European, ways. In fact, when I discussed my plans to skip the tours of museums and historic sites in Paris in order to visit my friends, one of my companions said I would be missing out on learning more about Hungarians. I immediately assented, since I was thinking about how I'd be missing their reactions to seeing French art and history. However, what my companion had meant was that I was missing an opportunity to learn about Hungary's and France's common European background in art and history, which at the time was less clear in Hungary because of the effects of the socialist period.

Unfortunately for Hungarians in the mid-1990s, as it has been historically, defining themselves in relation to Europe was necessarily an ambivalent project. This was the case because of the way Europe was used to refer to such traits as civilized, modern, and safe, while their own experiences kept telling them their lives were insecure and they had to catch up to modern Europe in terms of their political and economic systems. Clearly, to be insecure, as so many Hungarians in Szeged felt they were, was to be something other than European.

Action, Time, Service, and Selfhood

The most important things I learned on these trips were the meanings of "balkán" and "European" in the ways Hungarians imagine themselves and their nation. However, other aspects of being Hungarian in the world likewise became clearer to me while traveling outside the country's borders with groups of Hungarians. My own orientations to action, time, and service often conflicted with what I was experiencing with these Hungarian groups. Every time I became frustrated with my traveling companions or annoyed with the situation in which we found ourselves on these trips I had an opportunity to think about what aspect of my own identity was conflicting with theirs and vice versa. This traveling also clarified some experiences I had already had in Hungary but which had made no sense to me at the time.

One aspect of Hungarian identity that became clearer while traveling concerns Hungarian views of themselves as agents in the world. Prior to traveling outside of Hungary with groups of Hungarians I had certainly come across many differences between my own and many Hungarians' expectations and desires for independent action. This traveling, however, began to clarify for me why I was often uncomfortable in situations where my Hungarian acquaintances were not, and vice versa. U.S.-American ideologies construct an image of the individual as an active agent in the world, such that we exist and make the world meaningful through our own initiative (Natadecha-Sponsel 1993:49). Of course, in retrospect, the actions U.S.-Americans take may not always be the most beneficial way to approach a given situation, but this does not matter very much to the U.S.-American. I found that some Hungarians are not as action-oriented as U.S.-Americans. Their orientation to some situations, particularly when there is an authority figure present, is much more likely to be to wait for the authority to suggest or lead the action.

I experienced this tendency several times during the bus trip I took from Hungary to France. At several different times in the trip the group was given an opportunity to explore independently. Each time, I was the only one who wanted to walk around alone. In Strasbourg, for example, we were given forty-five minutes to do some exploring on our own after our tour guide had finished showing us the church and a few other sites. After more than twenty hours in a bus without air conditioning and speaking Hungarian for hours on end with more than a dozen strangers, I needed this short break to gather my thoughts, think in English, and get something to eat. I immediately set off on my own to explore and see a little bit more of the city. After approximately fifteen minutes I turned a corner to find the entire Hungarian group walking back towards the bus. The guide was going back because he was tired and had already seen Strasbourg many times before; the crowd was following him, they said, because without him they did not know where to go or what to see. Unfortunately for me, because everybody else was ready to go, I lost my opportunity to explore and was told my free time was over.

I found it a little odd that this group of strangers would prefer to stay together, even when given the chance to be independent of the group for just a little while. Equally odd were the questions I received each time the bus stopped and we were all given an opportunity to disembark. In a little town in the Loire Valley, where we were given a few free minutes to explore, I was followed by a group of Hungarians who wanted me to show them where they could buy the most inexpensive bread. At a gas station on our way back to the Paris hotel from the Loire Valley excursion, I was asked, before I even got off the bus, where my traveling companions could find a water spigot to refill their drinking bottles. I had never been to this little town, nor to the gas station, so I could not fathom why they thought I would know where to find these things. However, in both cases, I took action and found what they were looking for.

Even at the time, I realized traveling outside of their country was a different experience for Hungarians than for English-speakers. Even when we do not speak the local language, in a real pinch we can usually find someone who speaks a little of ours. Hungarians almost never have this luxury. At the same time, these examples also come from Hungarians who have chosen a bus tour as their preferred means of travel. Perhaps it is true that, regardless of nationality or citizenship, bus tours are organized for people who are more comfortable being followers. Nonetheless, these experiences while traveling only served to highlight for me something I had been trying to understand about Hungarians generally. For example, while teaching at a Budapest university, it was very difficult to draw my Hungarian students into any sort of discussion of the material. I spoke, they wrote it down. They did not expect learning to entail any sort of active participation on their part in the way my students at the University of the Pacific often do. I was also struck almost daily by Hungarians' general willingness to follow an authority "figure" whenever I stood at an intersection. Rather than assess for themselves when it was safe to cross the street, almost every person in Szeged would stand at the corner and wait for the traffic signal to allow them to walk. Without fail, I would be the only person crossing against the light, even if there were no cars in sight.

Another important aspect of people's different orientations to the world and to the people around them related to this action orientation concerns expectations about the use of time. In general, I found Hungarians are not as impatient as U.S.-Americans often can be. Certainly, I knew before my field-work that U.S.-Americans reify time and are very concerned with using it in ways they consider productive, or at least using it for themselves. I have also read enough ethnography to know that many other cultures experience the passage of time in very different ways (Geertz 1973). Yet I was still not prepared to meet with a temporal worldview in Hungary, an industrial, European society, so different from my own. This is not to say, of course, that all Hungarians are as patient as the people in the following examples, or that all U.S.-Americans are as impatient with their time as I am. However, the differences I experienced are important for what they say about people's assumptions about their place in the world.

These differences between Hungarian and U.S.-American orientations to time were made very clear at several moments on the Istanbul trip. The clearest example came on the final day, when the bus was so late returning to Istanbul to pick us up. My two traveling companions and I were disappointed to have to leave Istanbul after only three days, but as long as we were leaving we wanted to get underway to be able to return home on schedule. The entire group met back in the lobby of the hotel at 11:00 A.M. to find there was no bus and no explanation for the delay. By 11:30 the two impatient U.S.-Americans decided not to allow the delay to ruin our last day in Istanbul, so while the group of Hungarians, surprised by our frustration and anger, sat smoking in the hotel lobby surrounded by their many packages, we went out to find some lunch. Géza, understanding our frustration but not sharing it entirely, decided to stay behind with our luggage; I suspect he was also called upon by the other Hungarians to explain his companions' odd behavior. Once outside, Anne and I took a final stroll down some of the interesting little side alleys where we had seen veiled women hurrying away from the traffic of the main streets with their children or grandchildren and basement sweatshops where older men sat sewing whenever we passed by. When it began to rain a little bit we came back to the hotel, although the smoke inside drove us to stand outside underneath an awning. We watched a pack of shoeshine boys as they trapped tourists into receiving a shine by wiping a smudge of polish across the tops of their shoes as they walked by or stood under the awning to escape the rain.

Eventually, even the rain was not enough to keep us in or near the hotel. When it got close to 1:30 we set off again to stroll the neighborhood, vent our growing anger at the inconveniences of the trip, and talk about the differences in U.S.-American and Hungarian expectations and dispositions. Somehow they could sit calmly in the hotel doing nothing for hours on end while we became frustrated and angry in less than half an hour. We couldn't wander far from the hotel, for fear of being left behind, but we did use our last hour in Istanbul to spend our last Turkish lira and to taste a kind of pastry we had not tried before.

The bus arrived at the hotel around 2:30, just as we were returning to give Géza his piece of pastry, and we finally set off around 3:00. This last half hour was spent packing the bus with the shoppers' enormous packages. We were amazed at the amount and variety of their purchases; not only had they bought t-shirts, jeans, leather jackets, baby clothes, and jewelry but one woman had purchased a mountain bicycle for her grandson and another had purchased a stainless steel kitchen sink! We had been joking as we helped carry the smaller bags to the bus that some of the larger ones must have weighed more than we did. Anne joked that the shoppers must have bought everything but a kitchen sink; when the sink was carried out a little later we laughed so hard most of the anger at having our time wasted dissolved. We were still disappointed we had not been able to use the morning and early afternoon to venture further away from the hotel and see something new, but we had at least recovered enough so we could see the humor of the situation.

I was confronted with a similar situation on the bus trip from Hungary to France as well. We had already stopped earlier in the day to tour Strasbourg and were on the road, still an hour or two from Paris, when one of the tires blew out. While the passengers all stood along the side of the road watching traffic whiz by at 120 km/hour, our driver slowly changed into a pair of denim coveralls to change the tire. Unfortunately, at some point after he removed the nuts with the old tire and when he reached to put them back on with the new one, one of the nuts got lost. For the next hour everybody helped comb the area for the missing part. Again, everybody else on the trip simply accepted the situation and calmly helped look for the missing part while I grew cranky, tired, and frustrated with the waste of time. In the end, somebody did find the part and we were able to get moving again. However, I seemed to be the only passenger who wanted the driver to speed up both the repair work and his driving speed, in order to make up for the time wasted along the side of the road. I mentioned this to some of the others but they dismissed it as unnecessary: "We'll get there when we get there."

Indeed, in order to amuse themselves, and perhaps to make me feel better as well, my traveling companions started laughing and talking again about a t-shirt one of the women wore throughout the trip. As with much of the clothing imported into Hungary, this t-shirt had a saying written on it in English. Many of these kinds of shirts have the names of nonexistent sports teams or nonsense phrases written on them, but this one had a very clear message: "If you like sex and travel, then take a f**king hike!" Naturally, the moment I saw the t-shirt I understood its saying, despite the use of asterisks, and wondered if its owner likewise understood. I doubted it, since she didn't speak a word of English. So on the second day of our trip, during one of the stops, I decided to ask her about it. As I expected, she could not read the shirt's message and had purchased it because of the bright colors; the lettering was done in bright blue, red, yellow, and green. When I translated the saying, to the best of my ability given that I couldn't turn that verb into an adjective in Hungarian, she roared with laughter. She immediately told her companions who likewise roared and soon the entire bus was laughing and repeating my poorly-translated, but equally crude, version of this saying. When they once again started laughing and talking about this incident following the two-hour stop alongside the French highway it seemed significantly less funny to me than it did at first; yet, somehow, it maintained its humor for all of my companions.

I realized over the course of my fieldwork that many Hungarians have a different conception of themselves and their relationship with time than many U.S.-Americans. In the U.S., many people think of time as a thing they own. They can sell it to employers or spend it themselves, they can waste it or save it, but however they choose to use it, it is their possession and they become angry when someone else takes it away from them. U.S.-Americans do not like to stand in line at the grocery store or wait in traffic; these inactivities take time away from them and waste it. Many Hungarians, on the other hand, are much less concerned about this issue. Waiting for trams that do not come or in lines that do not move because the cashier is busy talking with an acquaintance do not frustrate them or anger them to the degree it does many U.S.-Americans. Time for many Hungarians is less an object to be owned than a way to divide day and night into units.

These differences between U.S.-American and Hungarian expectations about the use of time became frustratingly clear to me at times when I wasn't traveling as well. Every time I found myself standing with a crowd at the tram stop waiting for a tram that never came or came very late, or waiting with dozens of pedestrians, bicyclists, and automobiles for fifteen minutes at a railroad crossing with no train in sight, I wondered what made Hungarians so patient. I often found myself walking into town rather than waiting with the Hungarians for the tram, or ducking under the railroad barriers to cross, much as I did at empty intersections with red lights. In each of these cases, my experience told me to take action and stop wasting time by waiting for the late tram, the distant train, or the traffic signals. The Hungarians I was wait-ing with, however, never chose this route. They waited patiently and silently, most without even glancing at their watches as they did so.

Another lesson I learned from these trips about Hungarian identity con-cerns expectations about the service economy. Hungarians in the early and mid-1990s were not accustomed to being treated well by those they elected or paid to serve them. Whether as a legacy of forty years of socialism, a system dedicated to eliminating consumerism, or some other factor, at that time Hungarians did not expect their service economy to provide much service. In part, my frustration with the trams that did not run on certain days without any advance notice, or the cashiers who allowed people to stand in line while they socialized, is connected with my U.S.-American expectation that money buys service. My Hungarian acquaintances had fewer of these expectations. On the trip home from Istanbul, Anne and I spent much of our time planning the action we could take to get reimbursement from the travel agent who booked our trip, or at least preventing her from selling this trip to other tour-ists. We spoke with the other couple from Szeged about joining us when we went to complain to the agent. They did not exactly laugh at us but did say it was useless and there was nothing we could do. We imagined our confronta-tion with the agent: threatening her with negative publicity and demands for a refund. Géza allowed us to daydream for awhile, and did lead our little group into the agent's office, but in the end he too acknowledged it was use-less. There was nothing we could do.

I experienced moments on my bus trip to France, as well, when I felt I was not receiving the kind of service I paid for. I knew we would be traveling for more than twenty-four hours before our final destination, a hotel near Paris's DeGaulle airport. I thought I had packed an appropriate amount of food and beverage for the first few meals and that I would be able to go to a grocery store for later ones. In fact, I imagined everybody would need to do this during our stop in Strasbourg since the weak Hungarian forint would prohibit restaurant meals. The one thing I was correct about in these assump-tions was that nobody had planned on dining out. Instead, everybody else on this trip had brought enough food with them for the first three or four days! The only stops we made along the way were at highway rest areas. During the stop in Strasbourg we only had time to see a few sites, in an area devoid of markets, before we were herded back on to the bus. I did find one small cheese shop just across the street from where the bus was parked and man-aged to purchase a box of crackers and some cheese, but only by forcing the bus to tie up traffic as it waited for me. I expected that because I was paying for a vacation, steps would be taken to make me comfortable, including allowing me to buy food. The Hungarians had no such expectations.

I do not present these narratives with the intention of making value judg-ments or explicit comparisons with U.S.-Americans generally. Rather, I want to illustrate the ways in which contrast with the anthropologist's identity and orientation to the world provides one way to learn about the informants'.

Certainly there are many positive reasons for doing research in communities in which the researcher feels at home; however, there is a trade-off. Familiarity may allow the anthropologist working at home access to events and local knowledge the stranger may lack. At the same time, elements of the anthropologist-at-home's own culture that are taken for granted, such as its orientation to action, time, and otherness, may remain invisible without the benefit of cultural contrast. I am convinced that if my own orientation were not so different, I would not have noticed a Hungarian reluctance to rely upon the efficacy of individual action or their comfort with the passing of time.

Conclusion

In parts of this chapter I have digressed somewhat from my theme of insecurity and Hungarian national identity as imagined and experienced in Szeged. However, the discussions in this chapter are connected to my larger theme in various ways. First, Hungarians' concern with insecurity is made more understandable in light of an orientation to the world that does not emphasize action. Taking action, rather than being acted upon, may be the only way to succeed in the capitalist economy in which Hungarians have found themselves since 1990. The same might be said for an orientation to time. For better or worse, the rewards of the capitalist economy go to those who act, and who act quickly. Many Hungarians are not accustomed to either of these ways of being in the world, and this may very well contribute to their feelings of insecurity.

In the following chapter, I go back to my explicit discussion of the use of insecurity to characterize the Hungarian nation. I look at one specific incident that for the residents of Szeged came to exemplify the insecurities of the post-socialist era. The next chapter follows somewhat naturally from this one because the incident it addresses is meaningful to those in Szeged since it is said to exemplify the threat of "balkán" ideas, behaviors, and people. If anyone in Szeged had been unconvinced about the insecurity of their nation before 1994, the events of January 26th of that year seem to have convinced them.

CHAPTER 6

The Danger
Is Everywhere!

Introduction

On January 26th, 1994, the *Délmagyarország*, Szeged's largest and most popular daily newspaper, broke the story of the murders of Bálint Z. Nagy, his wife, and their two children. Z. Nagy, an extremely popular and well-known Szeged pastry chef, who owned and ran a shop across from Szeged's fountain in the center of town, was shot dead along with the rest of his family as they slept in the family's Szeged home. For weeks it was on most everyone's mind in Szeged; newspapers ran stories for months afterwards about the crimes themselves, crime in general, and related stories of Hungarians' insecurity. Radio and television news programs kept residents abreast of developments in the capture and subsequent charging of a Serbian suspect (who could not be tried for this case for lack of evidence, but who was later convicted of murder in a different Hungarian city). If people tried to forget about the events, they were reminded every time they ventured into the city center because the pastry shop remained closed for the rest of my time in Szeged. At first, the front steps of the shop were covered with flowers, cards, candles, and other expressions of sympathy. After many months in which nobody cleaned up the remains of this outpouring of grief, the dead plants and flowers stood as a sad memorial to the slain family. Every once in a while when I passed through the square I saw someone stop and look at the closed shop, perhaps remove his hat in sympathy or cross herself in prayer.

At the same time these murders generated grief, sympathy, and fear in Szeged, they also generated a huge public discourse on Hungarian insecurity that had effects on every aspect of public and private life. On the first day of coverage, the most anybody could do was speculate about the motive and praise Z. Nagy for his fine work, reputation, and success. As the months dragged on,

Z. Nagy's pastry shop several months after the murders.

more and more of the Szeged community contributed to the discourse that the murders generated. The fears I had heard about prior to these events had a public airing in Szeged's newspapers. Talk of insecurity went from being a vague, private expression of local experiences of the transition from socialism to a public discourse on Hungary and being Hungarian in the postsocialist world. This discourse became so significant that I believe it even affected the second free elections almost five full months after the murders were first reported. This is not to say this one event has characterized the entire period from 1989 through the present for people in Szeged, but during the time period this book covers, this was the most important public event they drew upon to illustrate their feelings concerning and experiences of the transition from socialism.

At the same time, I focus on this crime not only because it was so important to the people of Szeged but also because it was a defining moment of my fieldwork. At the beginning of January 1994 I celebrated the one-year anniversary of my arrival in Hungary and, because of this marker, began to worry about what I was going to write about when I got home. I knew I had loads of good fieldnotes, over a dozen notebooks full and several files on my laptop computer, but I didn't have any real way to organize them. I knew I was interested in what the Hungarian nation meant to these Hungarians, but that was it. I was feeling a little dejected about my fieldwork and nervous about eventually writing a dissertation based on it. Therefore, just after the New Year's holiday I decided to take a few days off from visiting people to sit in my room and read all of my fieldwork notebooks, take notes on my notes, and think. I found it extremely helpful to treat my own fieldnotes as if they were books from a library. After all, I had spent many years as an undergraduate and graduate student doing research papers based on the work of other anthropologists. I understood exactly what it took to dig out information from other people's research. I just needed to step back from these notes, read them as if they were not my own, and try to find some organizing principle. After three days of reading my own notes and thinking about them I finally began to understand that my acquaintances had been talking about security all year long. I certainly had not formulated a thesis yet, but it was a relief to know there was some pattern to all the information I had gathered up until that time. A couple of weeks later, when news of the Z. Nagy murders hit the local papers and became a topic of conversation with everyone I knew, I saw immediately this tragedy was the key symbol of my entire fieldwork.

I have already addressed many aspects of the Hungarian concern for security, such as the closure of networks, hoarding of food, and locking of gates, as well as the way foreigners, gardens, and garden work are implicated in Hungarians' feelings of insecurity. Nonetheless, I come back to the topic in this chapter in order to explain how these murders changed both Hungarians' sense of insecurity at the time and my understanding of this concept in Hungary. I also use this opportunity to present the voices of Hungarians other than my own informants in order to show that a concern with security was not limited to the people I happened to meet during my time in Szeged. The tidal wave of discourse these murders unleashed can be read in the words of law enforcement officials, government agents, media workers, and residents of Szeged who were interviewed each week by the local newspaper. In trying to depict the concerns and interests of this diverse group, as well as those of my informants and me, I draw upon a variety of sources in this chapter. The bulk of my information on the murders and the subsequent media blitz on security came filtered through my friends and acquaintances and through my reading of the *Délmagyarország*, Szeged's largest daily newspaper. (Unless otherwise noted, all citations concerning the Z. Nagy murders were taken from my own translations of articles in this paper.) However, I also had limited access to television and radio between January and July 1994 and pull from this knowledge as well. Throughout this chapter I draw upon these different sources, as well as my own experiences and the voices of my informants, to explore the meaning of security as it emerged publicly in Szeged in the first half of 1994.

Official Commentary

The tone of the discourse on these murders was largely set on the first day of newspaper coverage by statements from two public officials in Szeged. The first statement was made by a Szeged city council representative, who immediately blamed the crimes on foreigners: "It comes to mind that the young soldiers of the Serbian army, as civilians, came to Szeged by bus to shop with their 50 [German] mark allowance. Who could have predicted what they were up to in the meanwhile?" (1/26/94A:7). Echoing the sentiments of many in Szeged, he immediately blamed Hungary's "balkán" neighbors for importing violence and insecurity, even before there were any public indications that the murderer was a foreigner or group of foreigners. In an interview that also came out on the first day of the murders' coverage, the vice president of the Hungarian Parliament continued along the path forged for him by the Szeged councilperson. He said, "It should be obvious to everyone that we shouldn't only mutter over these questions [of security and governmental responsibility] at home but openly as well" (1/26/94B:7).

On the second day of media coverage, Szeged's police captain tried to counter these public statements and calm the mood in the city. He said, "The Z. Nagy affair is not the 'by-product' of the collapse of Szeged's public security . . . I can establish this with certainty" (1/27/94B:7). However, the fears that had been building locally for many months, as I knew from my research, were not to be assuaged by a few words from the officer. According to one reporter, "The Z. Nagy family tragedy is without change the main topic of conversation in Szeged. People keep guessing and *they consider the city's public security appalling*" (1/27/94A:7, italics in original). In response to this charge, the police captain replied, "*this is an individual event*, which is a sad tragedy. But this does not mean the city's public security is in critical condition" (1/27/94A:7, italics in original). Few people among my own acquaintances, among people interviewed for the newspaper, and among public officials trying to win the votes of these frightened and disillusioned Hungarians believed the police captain.

As a result, as far into the spring as March, the topic of security continued to dominate the media, as it had dominated my conversations with Hungarians for a year prior to the murders. For example, the Csongrád County police superintendent, Dr. László Salgó, wrote a series of five articles for the local paper on the security issue as it pertained to the city, county, and country as a whole. He addressed not only the responsibilities of the police, but also of lawmakers to enact legislation to help the police to do their jobs and of citizens to obey the laws and to participate in the social responsibility for creating security. On March 3rd, in the last of his five installments, he wrote, "It is possible to live in a Democracy only with the assurance of consolidated issues of public security" (3/3/94:13). In addition, he also stated many times that there exists in Szeged a vast difference between "objective security," as evident in police statistics and crime indices, and "subjective security" as felt by individuals (2/26/94:15). The day following this series, the minister of the interior at that time, Dr. Imre Kónya, supported this claim by providing statistics on the improving face of Hungarian crime fighting in 1993 (3/4/94:17). Over all, these essays presented a coherent ideology for the nation and state, based on the need to provide security for its members and citizens through democratic processes.

Unfortunately, for a population whose only contemporary experience with democracy had brought a significant amount of uncertainty and insecurity, the superintendent's words rang hollow. Like other officials, the superintendent was not listening closely enough to the local discourse the murders had instigated, nor had he correctly interpreted local constructions of Hungary and the Hungarian nation as insecure. Crime was not the only concern at the heart of the "subjective feelings of security" I had noted during my residence in Szeged and that were vented in the public venue during the long coverage of the Z. Nagy murders. My acquaintances spoke with me about crime, certainly, but they also talked extensively about economic uncertainties caused by unemployment, immigration, inflation, and the rollback of social services. Indeed, even when they spoke with me about crime, it was clear this topic was not only important in and of itself, but it served as a way to address many other forms of insecurity.

Crime Discourse

I found in Szeged even before the murders that discussions on crime and criminality were a regular part of many people's day-to-day conversations, both with me and with other Hungarians. In terms of actual criminal occurrences, perhaps their concerns were justified; Hungary may have seen a dramatic increase in crime between 1989 and 1994. Until 1988, between two and three thousand crimes per year were recorded by the sheriff's office in Csongrád County. The figure for 1992 was nine thousand (Délmagyarország 3/1/94:11). However, Hungarians were more free to report crimes to the police in 1992 than in the socialist era, when it was largely the state and its agencies that were committing what most Hungarians considered to be crimes against their fellow citizens (Csepeli and Örkeny 1992:7). Therefore, the actual crime figures for the years immediately before and after 1990 may actually be much closer to each other than the official figures indicate.

Nevertheless, continually talking about crime became one of the most common ways of expressing the overall insecurity the people of Szeged felt characterized them and their nation in the early and mid-1990s. When meeting new people, the first questions most people asked me concerned crime in the United States; I was even told by three different people that I should feel at home in Szeged because it is a "Little Chicago" with its own Capone. Others wanted to know if my life in the U.S. was like the world they saw on television shows like *Miami Vice* and *Kojak*. A few were even convinced they know what life is like in the U.S. from viewing Charles Bronson movies. I was told by Hungarians of the need for vicious guard dogs, and I saw for myself the dog schools in Szeged where Rottweilers, German Shepherds, and pit bulls are trained to attack intruders and to bark and snarl at strangers passing by on the street. The explanation always given to my queries about the gates and fences that surround every individual house in Szeged is a need for protection against criminals (see chapter 3). When I asked if this had always been true, I was told that in the past these fences were required to keep chickens, pigs, dogs, and other animals within courtyards. It is only since the start of the transition that they had been required to keep criminals out.

In addition to taking part personally in innumerable conversations concerning crime, I was told of many others. My landlady came home almost daily with tales of robbery or attempted robbery that acquaintances told her while they waited for a bus together or while they tended the flowers on their husbands' graves. Every Sunday evening, when she returned from her daughter's house, she also relayed stories her granddaughter told about her work in a Szeged grocery store. It seemed like every week the granddaughter had either caught a shoplifter or had to let one run from the store, since leaving the cash register unguarded would invite further crimes. Other acquaintances often told me about things they had heard about crimes in Szeged, such as that Z. Nagy and his family had been shot execution-style with one bullet each into the left eye. I never saw any mention of this rumor in the newspapers, yet it was a common conversation topic for many months. From what I could tell by questioning my acquaintances about their own interactions with other acquaintances, colleagues, and family members, the people of Szeged not only took advantage of the international audience they found in me to talk about crime, but also regularly talked about it amongst themselves.

In fact, after almost a year of hearing this kind of conversation over and over again I didn't take much notice anymore of the ways in which almost everyone at some point in our conversation introduced crime. I had become so used to the topic that my vocabulary included terms that occasionally surprised my language tutors, such as "*gyámhatóság*," the court of legal guardianship, and "*bűnsegéd*," a criminal accomplice. Most people who learn Hungarian as a second language, I was assured, do not learn this kind of vocabulary. But for my research purposes, discovering what was important to Hungarians, I had to understand the terms being used again and again to talk about themselves and their experiences. In many cases, these terms referred to crime, courts, and the police.

Eventually, I came to understand that my acquaintances were talking about far more than crime when they broached this topic in conversation; they were expressing economic, personal, and national insecurities. First, when they discussed their fears of losing their few material possessions, they were expressing economic insecurities of all kinds. Everyone who said to me their gate must remain locked at all hours of the day and night explained that the theft of a car or some other valuable would be too expensive to replace and they would have to learn to live without it. One of my landladies, who had very little in her home a criminal could resell, was as afraid for her house in general as well as for her few belongings. She spoke of the potential violation of her home by criminals as if it would have invalidated her ownership of the property and all of her husband's and son's work to build the home many years earlier. Most everyone said it had taken years to accumulate their few valued possessions and saw their potential loss as if it not only deprived them of the objects but also negated their efforts. Many people also pointed out how difficult it had become to survive in the economic climate of the mid-1990s and crime was just one of many factors that made life so uncertain and insecure in the postsocialist era.

Second, like economic insecurity, personal insecurity was often coupled with crime by Hungarians who were groping for ways to express their fears of the postsocialist world. For example, I was warned time and again not to be too trusting, to find out what people wanted when they invited me someplace or offered to help me in some way, not to offer English conversation practice in my own apartment but only in public places. The message was always that you don't know whom to trust and who is a potential criminal. This issue had become particularly important for Hungarian women, as I address in the following chapter. Women in Szeged became afraid for their physical well-being in ways Hungarian men did not. They felt unable to walk alone at night or in Szeged's parks and cemeteries even during the day; they felt unsafe in their own homes. One twenty-four-year-old woman told me how thankful she was that she, her husband, and their small child lived in a large apartment complex, surrounded by people in other apartments who could hear her scream for help rather than in a private home where she would be alone with her child during the day. Another young woman moved back into her parents' private home from her own apartment in the same neighborhood because of her fear of living alone. My retired landlady also spoke of her anxieties at passing strangers on the paths of the local cemetery when others weren't around to give assistance and of riding the bus after dark back into the city from her daughter's village half an hour away. Another woman, a seventy-three year-old-widow, mourned her inability to take walks in the evenings and, like most women, spoke often of the security of the past political system. "In the past we may have been able to travel to the West only once every three years, but we felt safe in our own home (*ház*), we could enjoy Szeged, things were better then."

Third, the security of Hungary as a small nation and state was also coupled with crime in many of these conversations. The open border policy adopted by Hungary in 1990 allowed thousands of Romanians, Serbians, and others from "balkán" countries further to the south and east to enter Hungary without a visa. These people, it was commonly believed in Szeged, were often criminals, ready to take advantage of Hungary's judicial, military, and demographic vulnerabilities. The quotation from the woman who stated that in the past Hungarians in Szeged felt safe in their own homes is particularly interesting for its double meaning with regard to her personal security and that of the nation as a whole. In Hungarian the word *ház* can mean both home, with regard to one's own private living space, and homeland or nation, the living space of all Hungarians. Like most Hungarian women, and many men as well, this woman considers herself unsafe both in her own home and in her nation. Criminals can break into any home, as the example of Z. Nagy and his family aptly shows, and foreigners can break into Hungary, as is evident from the number of foreigners in Szeged every day. Neither of these "homes" that once provided security for Hungarians was able to do so in the mid-1990s.

In addition to my acquaintances, the people of Szeged used crime to speak about many of the insecurities of postsocialist life more generally. For several weeks following the Z. Nagy murders, answers to questions posed to Szeged residents in the *Délmagyarország*'s "Question of the Week" column illustrated some of the ways Hungarians connected this specific crime with other insecurities. On January 27, 1994, a male worker in his fifties replied to a "Question of the Week" concerning the Z. Nagy murders, "Has hell broken loose?": "It's sad we have to live this way! You go to bed at night and you don't know whether or not you'll get up in the morning. . . . We are at mercy because anything can happen" (1/27/94C:4). Two weeks later, an unemployed woman replied to the question, "Do we need to be afraid in the city?" by connecting the economic insecurities of that period to a discussion on crime. She concurred with my acquaintances who had spoken with me privately by saying, "There wasn't so much violence in the old system. . . . The living was better, the material security. In the first place, the strengthening of the economy should be primary in improving public security" (2/10/94:4). A retired male manual worker responded to this question by talking about both personal and financial security: "I think everyone who has money can be afraid they'll break into your place. . . . They should take every preventative measure [such as] barred windows, they need alarms, they should hire bodyguards. They should pay attention and *lock everything possible*" (2/10/94:4, italics added). A second retired man answered this question by turning to an idealized image of the nation as his solution to the insecurities the murders represented: "We should look for solutions in our culture and upbringing because today's national values have totally disintegrated" (2/10/94:4).

The responses of three Szeged residents to the *Délmagyarország*'s question of the week on February 24, 1994, which asked, "Aren't you afraid of the blood bath?", further illustrate that the concerns of the local Szeged community went far beyond these specific crimes, and, indeed, crime itself. While the question clearly points to the grisly murders that occurred in Szeged, the responses, like those published earlier that winter, indicate the security issue went well beyond the crime sphere and time frame of the murders in the minds of many Szeged residents. A middle-aged lecturer began her response by acknowledging her fear of crime, "I've had enough of the violence you can experience today" (2/24/94:4). However, she soon moved on to other topics. Voicing her concern for the economy, she stated, "The city is filled with homeless people; there is no security," and, "Of course it was another world in the past, there was work, money, it was livable." A middle-aged bookkeeper concurred with the lecturer on her concern with unemployment and adds her own fear of "the large number of foreigners" (2/24/94:4). A young man, who at the time of his interview was working for a public relations firm, pointed to the problem that people "don't care for one another" and stated he would like to see people coming together again to combat the forces that are driving them apart (2/24/94:4).

In addition to the opinion pages in the local newspaper, the residents of Szeged had other public outlets for making explicit connections between crime and the insecurity of their personal, local, and national communities. On Thursday, February 3, 1994, Zoltán Király, one of Szeged's representatives in Parliament, planned a "quiet demonstration" (2/2/94:16) to "protest against the fear" and to begin "a peaceful battle against the takeover [of Szeged] by the underworld" (2/4/94:1). Instead, the 400–500 person march down the main pedestrian streets of Szeged turned into a public arena for frustrated Hungarians to air their concerns. The shouts that were recorded in the *Délmagyarország* the following day include a concern with crime, "Bring back the death penalty!", "Who defends the little guy on the street?" (2/4/94:3), as well as other concerns. Expressing the frustration with national government felt at the local level, one person asked, "Where has Zoltán Király been up until now?"; another wanted to know, "What's this, campaigning?" (2/4/94:3). The last printed jeer addressed the economic insecurity felt by many Hungarians since the beginning of the transition. Someone suggested the minister of the interior and other members of Parliament "should try themselves to live on 8 thousand [forints] a month!" [at the time, about US$80] (2/4/94:3).

Such diverse communities in Szeged as the local membership of the Hungarian National Trade Union Organization (MSzOSz), the Forrás Management Club, and a meditation group also participated in the production of a public discourse on crime and security during the months of January, February, and March 1994. The Szeged branch of the Trade Union used the newspaper to call all residents and officials in Szeged to participate in the Z. Nagy funerals and to "do everything possible so that Szeged, the city of sunshine, doesn't turn into the city of shadow and crime" (1/28/94B:7). The Forrás Management Club took the opportunity of an open forum to raise the security issue from a number of different perspectives. They invited a psychologist, the main police speaker on crime prevention, and representatives from several security services to address their group on the ways both public and private security can be improved (2/11/94:7). A representative from the meditation group stated in the *Délmagyarország*, "If one in ten people in Szeged practiced transcendental meditation, the crime rate would go down" (2/17/94:6). The unidentified expert also claimed that individuals who practice this form of relaxation improve their possibilities for economic and business success, as well as the physical condition of their bodies.

While crime is certainly important in all of these discourses, other factors for the perceived insecurity are also very clearly articulated in the words of my acquaintances, the newspaper's respondents, the participants in the demonstration, and the organizers of these events. Indeed, all of the issues that had been central to the experiences of those in Szeged as they attempted to answer for themselves what it means to be Hungarian in the postsocialist world, emerged in the public forum of the local newspaper and a variety of public events. Economic, physical, and national security emerged as issues that not only characterized local community experiences of the transition but also were used by public officials and corporations to attract votes and customers.

Exhaustion Discourse

Whereas crime served as the primary idiom through which the people of Szeged spoke of their insecurities, it was not the only one. Before I left the United States to begin my work in Hungary, I was warned by many Hungarian-Americans that if I asked a Hungarian how he or she is, I should expect a complete and truthful answer; I should not expect the standard U.S.-American answer of "fine." Instead, I found Szeged to possess its own standard exchange: "How are you?" "Tired." The reasons given for this permanent state of exhaustion varied: too much work or studying, staying up late to listen to music or watch television, inability to sleep. However, when I probed more deeply into the source of their tiredness the discussion invariably turned to security.

While Hungarians did have one of the longest work weeks in Europe in the late 1980s (around sixty-seven hours per week) (Schöpflin et al. 1988:25), in the early to mid-1990s, the worry that their work would disappear or wouldn't pay enough to live on were the primary reasons for this response. I was told time and again that fear, stress, and insecurity on all levels leave people in a state of exhaustion, but at the same time, unable to rest or sleep properly. Some of the most telling explanations I received are, "It's not from work that everyone is tired, but the anxiety." "We worked hard in the past, too, but there was security in it. It's the insecurity, fear, instability that people always have on their minds that is so exhausting." "It's not the work but the petty things on my mind." "At the end of the day I just want to escape into my flat, watch a little television, maybe read a little, and sleep." For many Hungarians, the freedoms they won in the postsocialist era, such as the freedom to be unemployed, uninsured, and homeless, turned out to be just as anxiety-provoking as the lack of freedoms of speech, religion, and travel of the socialist era. This exhaustion not only has affected Hungarians as individuals, but also social networks and families as well, as I addressed earlier. While being Hungarian in the mid-1990s inevitably meant being tired, this exhaustion was a symptom of a larger phenomenon, the perception by many Hungarians that they and their communities, both local and national, were insecure.

One response to this perception on the personal level was to focus on the body. While few people were actually willing to break the habits and customs of generations of Hungarians—to quit smoking and drinking, cut fat from the diet, begin an exercise program and lose some weight—most everyone spoke about ways one or more of these programs to help the body could also alleviate fatigue. One particularly astute Hungarian firm realized this trend and used it to their advantage in marketing an expensive brand of supposedly U.S.-American vitamin supplements. For several weeks in the autumn of 1993 many people wanted to know if I understood the tremendous benefits of a particular vitamin in boosting energy. Few were daunted by the fact that I had never heard of the brand until I came to Hungary and everyone who asked me about these vitamins purchased at least one formula that was supposed to boost energy, aid sleep, or both. The many agendas people discussed for securing the body against fatigue, including these vitamins, various medications, exercise, meditation, and losing weight, all served as ways to channel their desire for security on all levels. However, like the keys that never get removed from the vicinity of the lock to provide real security, this discourse on improving the body rarely moved beyond the world of discourse into the world of action to provide real security against personal affliction.

Hoarding

Unlike physical fitness programs or changes in diet, an important course of action many Hungarians did take to protect themselves from insecurity in the mid-1990s was to maintain a large stockpile of food. During the socialist period Hungarians were always, with the exception of the end of 1956 and beginning of 1957, assured of a regular, affordable supply of basic foodstuffs. The stories Janine Wedel told with regard to standing in Polish food lines in the early 1980s, only to find the store had no bread, meat, or milk (1986), or Verdery for Romania (1992), are foreign to Hungarians. Everyone in Szeged whom I asked about food lines or shortages during the socialist era laughed at me; older people often told stories about having to trade with village relatives for food during World War II but no one could remember any shortages in Szeged since that time. Because of these responses, as well as their assurances that they did not hoard food during the socialist era, I found it very odd to be shown people's pantries, with many shelves of flour, sugar, coffee, and jars of preserved fruits and vegetables.

When I began to ask questions I soon discovered, although they did not feel the need to hoard food during the socialist era, many of them did in 1993 and 1994. One man said, "Hungarians today fear starving, so they keep deep freezers packed with pork." Another woman explained that in 1991 the price of meat skyrocketed and many people she knows went to Austria to buy deep freezers and now have them filled with meat. "They like the security of the freezer full of meat," she said. When I first moved in with one of my landladies in November 1993 she had a few bags of flour in the pantry, just in case something happened and she had to bake her own bread. By the time I moved out in July 1994, she had close to 100 pounds of flour; she assured me that her daughter had even more because she would have to bake for five people. They had both been slowly storing up the flour as they watched prices rise over that six-month period and began to fear their ability to afford the life-giving Hungarian bread. Another Szeged acquaintance kept both flour and sugar stored in her summer kitchen, an area behind the garage in which she stores provisions and her husband prepares chicken feed. At one point during my time in Szeged the media announced a sharp rise in coffee prices and for several days afterwards many people I know spent their spare time scouring the stores and markets for the old, cheaper coffee. My landlady bought coffee not just for herself but also more than twenty pounds of it for her granddaughter's wedding the following summer.

People in Szeged in 1993–94 were not taking chances with rising prices and potential shortages. One of the first things I learned about Hungary upon my arrival was that 1993 was the first time in decades Hungary had to import grain for bread. People were shocked and frightened. As I argued in chapter 4, one of the constants in Hungarian identity since the mid-nineteenth century has been an association with agriculture. The loss of agricultural autonomy evident in the need for foreign imports forced a reevaluation of all that it means to be Hungarian. For many years of the socialist era, Hungarians separated themselves from the other nations and states held within the Soviet sphere of influence and identified with the idea of "being the 'most comfortable barrack in the camp'" (Markus 1982:91). Part of this comfort had to do with the reassurances Hungarians had of always having enough to eat. It was unnecessary to rush to the store or market for a particular item, or to hoard it away once you found it, because it would always be available and affordable. By the time I arrived in Szeged in January 1993 this sense of security was gone. It continued to be true that a large assortment of domestic and imported food items were available; it was no longer true that everyone could afford them. People started stockpiling and storing basic items such as flour and meat in ways that, according to my acquaintances, would have been unimaginable a decade earlier.

The Nation as Imagined by the Szeged Community

The fears for personal and material security that are so evident in the words and deeds of many Hungarians in Szeged provided the concepts with which this population came to imagine the nation as a whole in the early and mid-1990s. This is not only a connection made by me as an anthropologist, who analyzes information as an outsider, but it is also a connection made by many Hungarians as well. For example, the mayor of Szeged said at the beginning of the Z. Nagy murder crisis, "We need to acknowledge that Szeged has become a transit city of a transit country, which is subjecting us to increased danger" (1/28/94A:7). Rather than naming a new problem, however, the mayor was just stating publicly something many in Szeged had long felt. Indeed, many people in Szeged believed the problems from which their community was suffering in the postsocialist world, such as crime, exhaustion, and economic disorder, were the result of the city's location on Hungary's border with "balkán" countries. Many felt the opening of the borders in 1990 and the thousands of visitors from these adjoining countries who entered the city on a daily basis had turned Szeged into a crossroads for international criminals from all over the former Soviet Union and "balkán" regions.

It was largely these concepts that members of the local Szeged community used to imagine the Hungarian nation as a whole. Hungary was in the same position as Szeged; crime, exhaustion, and economic disorder were plaguing the Hungarian nation and state because of its location on the margins of Europe, the border between Europe and the "balkán" regions. When the wars that plagued the former Yugoslavia began, wealthy and entrepreneurial Yugoslavian citizens began to flock into Szeged to shop, both for themselves and to sell on the black market. In the early and mid-1990s, instead of being grateful for this influx of foreign tourists, their hard currency, and the overall positive effects this commerce had on Szeged's economy, many people in Szeged felt overwhelmed and threatened by these shoppers.

Visitors from the former Yugoslavia and Romania were spoken of and treated as invaders rather than as tourists. Rather than seeing themselves as lucky to live near the border and benefiting from the flow of foreigners who came to Szeged daily, many people preferred to complain of the lines in stores and the rudeness of foreigners. The proliferation of advertisements and notices sprouting up in Serbo-Croatian were spoken of as signs of accommodation to a foreign invasion rather than as entrepreneurial acumen, which was not true of signs and menus in German and English. Even after the imposition by the Serbian government of large, hard-currency, exit duties drastically cut the numbers of foreigners entering from the south to approximately 42,500 daily (Délmagyarország 5/7/94:3), the people of Szeged continued to say that their city and their nation were at risk from these foreign elements.

Many people in Szeged feared the presence of these foreigners foreshadowed a repeat of the events that immediately followed World War I. At that time, military loss to the Allies, a change of political system from monarchical empire to socialist state (Hungary had a communist revolution in 1919 that was overthrown less than a year later), and weakened borders allowed both Serbia and Romania to invade Hungary and leave troops positioned in and around Szeged for several years. Szeged and the Hungarian nation and state were seen to be at risk of being swallowed up by neighbors with powerful international allies. Drawing on this collective memory, Hungarians in Szeged in the early and mid-1990s feared that ideological loss, system change from socialist state to democracy and capitalism, and open borders would precipitate another foreign invasion, this time in the form of "balkán" tourists and businessmen interested in destroying their Hungarian nation and culture. One woman who grew up in the interwar period and remembers the havoc of the early 1920s said in 1993, "Today in Hungary is like after Trianon: Hungary was alone at the end of the Monarchy; we didn't know what would happen to us. It's the same today. The danger is everywhere!" Other people who are much too young to remember this period of Hungarian history likewise pointed to their nation in the 1920s when searching for a reference point with which to compare the early and mid-1990s. This time, however, they feared neither their city nor their nation would be as lucky as they were earlier in the century. From their local experiences of fear and insecurity, as well as a local construction of past events, the population of Szeged produced a national ideology based on shared insecurities.

Security as a Public Issue

Until January 1994 this multifaceted discourse on security was primarily private. The answers I received to questions about holidays, friends, health, Szeged, the economy, politics, and just about everything else invariably broached the issue of security. When I met with Hungarians for interviews, planned get-togethers, or impromptu meetings, the topic often turned to the concept of security. Likewise, I often overheard conversations on buses and trams, in the markets and stores, and on the streets that indicated the topic was much more widespread than my network of acquaintances. The people of Szeged spoke of little else in 1993–94. Security was the master narrative circumscribing local life and private discursive events; security defined what it meant to belong to the Hungarian nation, at least as it was experienced in Szeged.

After the murders of Z. Nagy and his family began to dominate the local newspaper, television, and radio, this concern with security became a public issue as well as a private one. The media, politicians, and others with the ability to speak to the nation and state as a whole began using the topic of security for their own purposes. In the spring of 1994, national elections provided Hungary's most well-known political figures the opportunity to reach out to local communities and speak to them about their plans to bring back Hungarian security. Advertisements in Szeged for many of the largest political parties used the issue of security to woo voters. For example, the phrase used in much of the MDF, Magyar Democratic Forum, campaign advertising was "Certain steps—Steady future." In Hungarian, the word "certain," *biztos*, comes from the same root as the word for security, *biztonság*, so this phrase not only ties the MDF campaign to images of the future, but it also defines that future as one that will be secure or certain if Hungarians vote for this party.

In the same way, the newspaper and poster campaign of the SzDSz, Alliance of Free Democrats, also relied heavily on one phrase. Rather than one that focused voters' attention on some nebulous future, however, the SzDSz campaign forced voters to consider the issues and asked them to "trust" in

Alliance of Free Democrats' (SzDSz) campaign poster, Szeged, March 1994.

their solutions. The phrase "I trust in it/him/her" (all the same word in Hungarian) was repeated on many of the different advertisements that appeared before the first round of voting and referred to specific SzDSz plans and candidates. Like the MDF's *biztos*, the word for trust as used in this phrase, *bízom*, also comes from the same root as the word for security.

While these two parties used catch-phrases that reminded voters of their perceived insecurities, FIDESZ, the Young Democrats, inundated readers of Szeged's newspapers and billboards with local candidates' personal histories and the party's ideas for Hungary's future. One particular essay, "Freedom and Security," published in a series of *Délmagyarország* advertisements entitled "Let's Talk About the Basics," seemed to speak directly to the people of Szeged and their concern for security. In that essay the FIDESZ candidates claimed,

> FIDESZ is a national, committed, moderate liberal party. Our basis is freedom. Freedom of the individual, the family, the public sphere, the country and the nation. Freedom, however, cannot develop without security. Neither can the individual nor the community. The citizen's freedom can come about if we don't need to fear criminals, nor the intervention of government bureaucracy, nor existential security. For the sake of voters it's most important we guard and fulfill our freedom and security. . . . Security for the country. . . . Security for the citizens.

It seemed as if FIDESZ was the party to support if you wanted the concept of security to be important in Parliament for the next four years. However, only about seven percent of voters in Szeged and in Hungary generally agreed.

Most Hungarians at that time selected MSzP, the Hungarian Socialist Party, as the party they most wanted to lead them and their country during the 1994–98 electoral period. The majority of this party's campaign material in Szeged relied on the phrase "*Megbízható megoldást*," which encompasses a variety of meanings having to do with their experience and past, "The reliable/trustworthy/authoritative solution." Most everyone in Hungary associated MSzP with the former socialist system, including its stability and forty years of political experience. They also associated MSzP with Kádár's paternalist promises of both existential and public security, and his ability to provide these for many years. Therefore, the Socialist Party, as it existed during the elections of 1994, embodied the good, secure aspects of Hungary's past, when Hungarians could think of themselves as "the most comfortable barrack in the camp." At the same time that many Hungarians associated MSzP with a secure past, this party also represented the reform wing of the former Socialist Worker's Party. These were the people who ousted Kádár in 1988 when he became too old and ideologically entrenched to rule effectively, who tore down the barbed wire and opened Hungary's borders to the West, and who ushered in the new era of freedom. As early as October 1993, one young man, a FIDESZ supporter, said to me he thought the Socialists would do quite well in 1994 because they were the people who had begun the reforms but had subsequently been swept from power. He thought people would bring them back because of their past record.

A final reason for the MSzP victory was that they were seen as free from blame for the insecurities of the first four years of the transition, having been outside of both the coalition government and the organized opposition. The young man I cited above also spoke of their "clean" record with regard to the dishonesty and corruption of the period 1990–1993. In order to emphasize their understanding of the plight of ordinary Hungarians, party leader and future prime minister Gyula Horn's message throughout the campaign was, "As the party that cares for your problems, we will be the government of social dialogue. National-level negotiations will be the means *for you to educate a socially responsible government* about your sufferings, which we will devise measures to treat" (Stark and Bruszt 1998:172, italics in original). Therefore, although many parties joined in the public outcry concerning security in the spring of 1994, the party with which voters had experienced security in decades past won the election and went on to head the coalition government.

Conclusion

According to Hungarian crime statistics and other information, members of the Szeged community may have been able to engage these politicians and media leaders in a discourse on security long before January 1994. In general, the period between 1963 and the early 1980s was marked in Hungary by "solid existential security, gradual improvement of living conditions, and steady economic growth" (Kis 1989:236). But by the mid- to late 1980s foreign debt, the largest per capita in eastern and central Europe, and economic stagnation had brought this period to an end. It has been estimated that the official inflation rate of seventeen percent for 1988 was really closer to twenty-five or thirty percent (Schöpflin et al. 1988:25) and that at the time "from one-fourth to two-fifths of the people . . . live[d] below the poverty line" (Schöpflin et al. 1988:27). Schöpflin, Tőkés, and Völgyes also cite the health care system, housing shortages, and hopelessness as problems that eroded this guaranteed existential security prior to the system change in 1990. Indeed, according to statements from many of the people I know in Szeged, it was a desire for improved economic security rather than any desire for freedom or democracy that moved them to support the political changes of 1988–90.

In the crime sphere, as well, Hungarians had begun to experience loss of security long before the Z. Nagy murders. In the words of the minister of the interior in the spring of 1994, after the Z. Nagy murders and the resulting outcry on security began to be addressed by politicians, "In the past decade the number of crime events has gone up significantly" (Délmagyarország 3/4/94:17). In Szeged, people had been talking about crime continuously for at least a full year prior to the murders. However, none of these factors, no national event or local belief, including the death in office in December 1993 of the first democratically elected, postsocialist prime minister in Hungary, was able to generate the kind of public response the murder of Bálint Z. Nagy and his family did. These murders hit all of the nerves that had been left raw and vulnerable throughout Hungary during the late 1980s and early 1990s and in so doing made security a public issue as well as a private one.

First, the murders spoke to people's fears for their own and Hungary's economic future, namely, the value of their work and the inability of honest, law-abiding people to get ahead. It was conjectured from the very beginning that Z. Nagy, a life-long Szeged resident and private business owner, a real Hungarian success story, had somehow become a victim of the mafia, either through smuggling, arms dealing, or simply refusing to pay the "protection money" demanded by them. At the same time that he and his family ran one of the most successful small shops in the city, they were also living in the "Wild East," a Hungarian comparison of themselves with the gun-slinging and out of control U.S.-American Wild West. The popular belief in Szeged was that the Z. Nagy family was working hard to prosper, despite the increasing inflation and stagnation of wages that financially burdened most Hungarians, and became the victims of envious or greedy criminals who took advantage of their prosperity. The fact they may have had ties to the mafia that contributed to their success was not lost on most people, but was dismissed as merely a fact of life for Hungarians like Z. Nagy who wanted to be capitalists.

Second, the murders spoke to Hungarians' fears for themselves and their own property. Z. Nagy and his wife and children were shot in cold blood as they slept in their family home in Szeged. The locks, dogs, and security system that they, and most people in Szeged, relied on to keep them safe and secure failed the ultimate test. In addition, a primary symptom of the insecurity of the current era is fatigue, difficulty sleeping, and a general sense of physical decrepitude. The bodies of the members of this family were the victims of the ultimate abuse as they tried to rest and combat their own fatigue. No vitamin supplement or course in transcendental meditation would have protected them from the violence.

Third, these murders spoke to general fears for the security of the Hungarian nation. Even before the links had been made between these murders and similar killings in Subotica, a city just over the Serbian border, and a Serbian citizen was taken into custody, most everyone agreed the crimes had been committed by a foreigner, probably a "balkán." The information that emerged later just confirmed what people had already come to believe: Hungarians, the people of Szeged especially, were at risk from the multitude of foreigners who enter the country on a daily basis. That these events occurred in Szeged, a border city, reinforced the identification of the Hungarian nation as a border nation that is put at risk by its geographic placement in Europe, much as Szeged was put at risk due to its geographic location in Hungary.

In the next chapter I reexamine these discourses about insecurity, as well as Hungarians' experiences with them, in the postsocialist era. Rather than looking at individuals as Hungarians, however, I look at them as Hungarian women and Hungarian men. The view of the Hungarian nation as insecure is built upon already taken-for-granted ideas about gender. The representation of the nation as a weak woman, the representation of its feminine members as insecure, and the actual experiences of these women in Hungary help to legitimate and naturalize the view of the nation as insecure in the postsocialist era.

CHAPTER 7

Security and the Gendered Nation

Introduction

In this chapter I want to go back and reexamine through a gendered lens some of the ethnographic details I have presented throughout the book regarding the idea of insecurity and its connection to the Hungarian nation in the minds of many in Szeged. This analysis is necessary for two reasons. First, different members of the Hungarian nation experience insecurity differently based on their gender. For example, a woman walking in Szeged alone at night is probably worried about robbery, rape, and harassment, while a man in the same position may only be worried about robbery. At the same time, women's and men's work in gardens and their social networks, and the ways each of these activities are connected to security in many Hungarian minds, also are affected by their place in Hungary's gender system. In each of these cases, I argue that the intersection of ideas about gender, security, and nation create different, gendered opportunities for experiencing the self as a participant in the imagined national community.

Second, while appearing to be a set of natural differences based on biological sex, gender is actually a culturally constructed system of rank. Indeed, gender in most societies is the most naturalized hierarchical difference, meaning that the significations of masculinity and femininity in any given context are so taken for granted that they are unquestionable to those who have been enculturated into their system. In addition, because of their apparent naturalness, gendered representations provide extremely powerful images and beliefs to which other cultural systems can be connected. For example, even though women have joined military units in many different times and places throughout the world, the concept of the "military" in most societies (but not all) is still a masculine one. Similarly, even when men stay home as the primary caregivers, the private sphere is still feminine in most societies. Neither of these definitions is natural; they are both the result of a gender system that defines aggression as masculine and nurturance as feminine.

Like the military and the home, the nation is also an institution infused with naturalized gender beliefs. However, unlike the military and the home, the "gender" of nations is more ambiguous and fluid. For example, the nation in Russia often is represented as the feminine "Mother Russia," while in Germany it is primarily a masculine "Fatherland." In addition, the gendered representations of a nation may be masculine in some circumstances, as in Uncle Sam to represent a militarized United States, and feminine in others, as in the Statue of Liberty to represent a nurturing and welcoming United States. In Hungary, the nation was gendered in the mid-1990s by the images and incidences used by its members to represent and exemplify the imagined community and its members. In my experience, the images and incidences Hungarians used were largely ones that feminized the nation in order to make it seem weak and vulnerable in relation to its neighbors.

Throughout this chapter I examine both the ways national and gendered ideologies constrain and enable individual experiences and the ways individual experiences contribute to the construction of national and gendered ideologies. I need to examine both sides of these processes because, as I argued in the book's introduction, I believe ordinary members of nations are not merely cultural consumers but cultural producers as well.

Experience and Ideology

Hungarians in the mid-1990s employed taken-for-granted gender categories to naturalize the idea that their postsocialist nation was at risk from foreign, specifically "balkán," forces. The seemingly natural idea in Hungary that women are weak, vulnerable, and in need of men's protection formed the basis of a metaphor used by many Hungarians to talk about their nation. One way this metaphor emerged during my fieldwork was with the use of crime victims as representations of the nation as a whole. This was a gendered discourse in that crimes in which Hungarian women were the victims often served as a way for Hungarians to represent how insecure their nation was to each other, as well as to the anthropologist who studied them. Crimes in which Hungarian men were victims were rarely, if ever, used to discuss the nation as a whole.

For example, following the murder of Z. Nagy and his family I found the greatest shock and horror was expressed over the fact that his wife was murdered along with him (West 1997). This was the case even though the murders had made it obvious that everyone in Hungary was equally at risk of violent crime. Everyone with whom I spoke about these events asked me immediately if I realized his wife had been murdered. With the exception of one young acquaintance, who attended school with Z. Nagy's son, no one focused on the murder of the two children. I found this very odd considering the importance Hungarians place on children, as well as the outrage often expressed in other countries whenever a child or group of children gets caught in the line of fire during bouts of adult violence. Nevertheless, in this case, only the murder of Z. Nagy's wife was chosen time and again to point to the risks of being Hungarian.

This woman's murder also rekindled many people's interest in crimes committed against three other Hungarian women. The first case was of a young woman who was kidnapped from a town north of Szeged two and a half years earlier. This case was particularly interesting to me since everyone who spoke of it did so using present tense verbs. I was very confused about the whole affair; I could not find mention of a kidnapping in the newspaper, yet everyone with the exception of a fellow U.S.-American anthropologist and me seemed to know about it and want to talk about it. One day, when my landlady again began talking about the murder and kidnapping as if they were the same case, I finally asked about the specifics of the crime, such as when the woman had been snatched. Much to my amazement, she told me she could not remember exactly when it happened, but it was probably some-time in 1991 or 1992! It wasn't until later, after I had heard dozens of people speak about these cases as examples of Hungarian insecurity, that I realized that for my landlady, as well as many other Hungarians in Szeged, this kid-napping and the murder of Z. Nagy's wife in January 1994 were one case. They were both just representative of the larger problem: the insecurity of the Hungarian people and their nation.

There were two other "crimes" I heard discussed frequently in Szeged at this time. One of these concerned the Hungarian woman who was allegedly raped by a Serbian border guard so the shopping bus on which she was travel-ing could pass through on its way to Istanbul. The other concerned the Hun-garian woman who died of a heart attack on one of these buses after what were assumed to be Turkish criminals had stolen all of the goods she was bringing back to Hungary to sell. I addressed both of these "crimes," for which I never found any proof, in some detail in chapter 5. However, I men-tion them here as well because they serve the same discursive function as talk about the murder of Mrs. Z. Nagy and the kidnapping. In all four cases, the important aspect for many Hungarians was that they were crimes committed against Hungarian women by foreign men. Even when the identity of the perpetrator was unknown, as was the case in all but the alleged rape, the Hungarians with whom I spoke referred to them as foreign, specifically "balkán," men.

There was yet another confrontation between a Hungarian woman and a foreign man that occurred on my trip to Istanbul which, for the people on the trip anyway, became a temporary symbol of their nation's insecurity. Hungar-ians who wanted to enter Turkey in 1993 and hadn't done so prior to arrival were required to purchase a visa at the border before they were allowed to go through immigration. All of the Hungarians with whom I was traveling, except the tourist couple from Szeged, had purchased theirs ahead of time and thus could enter Turkey together. This couple, however, was not able to enter with the rest of the group because they were standing in a different line to purchase their visas. When they attempted to go through immigration a few minutes later, after receiving the proper visa, the border guard refused to admit them until he spoke with our tour guide. He required ten German marks to allow the man into the country, but the woman's entry required a bit more. The guard signaled for our guide to enter his booth and when she did he raised up her sweater, stroked her behind, and then sent her out. The price for one Hungarian woman to enter Turkey was the harassment of another. While the Turkish guard did not commit rape or murder, he did take advantage of a Hungarian woman and embarrass her in front of her own tour group and anybody else who happened to be looking into the glass booth. For the Hungarians who were looking on, this act was a very visible symbol of Hungary's and Hungarians' powerlessness in relation to their aggressive neighbors. As one of my fellow travelers said, "Anikó [our guide] is being treated like Hungary; the Turk can do whatever he wants to her."

In early June 1994 yet another woman became the victim of a crime in Szeged, which again brought Mrs. Z. Nagy, the kidnapping victim, and all the other female crime victims back to the surface of my acquaintances' consciousness. The background of this reemergence is that someone planted a bomb on the steps of one of Szeged's Roman Catholic churches during the night and the following morning an elderly woman placed the package in a nearby garbage can. Later in the morning of the same day the bomb exploded, destroying the garbage can and injuring a younger female passerby. No one was killed, no serious property damage was incurred, and no individual or group claimed responsibility for the bomb.

What is most interesting about this event is the contrast with a similar event in Budapest. Just about a week after the Szeged bombing, a bomb exploded at the entranceway to the Hungarian Parliament building. In the letter claiming responsibility, a Hungarian right-wing nationalist group stated they were protesting the parliamentary elections and would continue to protest the election of MSzP in May 1994 by killing every representative who wanted to lead the nation away from traditional Hungarian values. The church bombings, plural because a church in Subotica, Serbia was bombed on the same morning as the Szeged church, remained unsolved. Strangely, despite the rhetoric of hate and the threats of continued violence made by the Hungarian group, it was the Szeged events rather than those in the capital that joined the ranks of the murder of Mrs. Z. Nagy, the kidnapping, and these other crimes, as representations of the insecurity of Hungary and Hungarians. Of course, the fact that this was a local event was somewhat responsible for the heightened awareness in Szeged. However, this does not explain the connections made between the bombing of a church, which in actuality only damaged a trash can, the injuries to one woman, and the insecurity of the nation as a whole. Certainly the bombing of the Parliament building and threats to many of its members would seem to make a stronger case for the nation's insecurity, despite its distance from the people in Szeged.

Two characteristics of the Szeged bombing make it a better symbol for the insecurities of the nation than the one in the capital. First, the Szeged bombing was linked by all who spoke of it with the simultaneous bombing in Serbia. The Szeged bomb was seen as much more threatening to the nation because of the connection with the uncivilized and dangerous "balkáns." The bombing of the parliament building and threats to its members were made by other Hungarians, who are rarely spoken of as the cause of the nation's insecurities. Second, this bomb injured one woman and had the potential of harming the elderly woman who had found the package in the first place. Like Mrs. Z. Nagy, these women served as more salient representatives of national insecurity than the mostly male members of parliament. The injuries sustained by the female passerby, because of her being in the wrong place at the wrong time, represented to many in Szeged the injuries being sustained by the nation because of its location in the wrong place in Europe.

In addition to these specific cases, both women and men in Szeged told me of the dangers for women of walking alone at night, of visiting cemeteries and parks during the daytime, and of living independently. Many people warned me of the risks I was taking in walking home after dark, even when I was with a female acquaintance. Concerned Hungarians walked with me or gave me a ride home on several occasions. After the Z. Nagy murders and the resulting increase in fear, the concern for me and for women in general increased dramatically. And with each warning to be careful, I was once again reminded of the insecurity of the nation as a whole.

The result of these kinds of discourses in 1993–94 was that it was taken for granted that the Hungarian nation, like its women, was weak and vulnerable. Mutually reinforcing gender and national ideologies, constructed around the idea of insecurity, created a situation in which Hungarian women and the Hungarian nation were seen to be at risk, primarily due to foreign criminals invading from the south and east. In their imaginings of postsocialist Hungary, both women and men used crimes against the bodies of Hungarian women, both real and potential, to illustrate the insecurity of the nation. This was the case despite the fact that women, men, and children were all crime victims at this time. At every opportunity, the people of Szeged were intimating that the body of their nation was being attacked through the bodies of their women (West 1997).

Ideology and Experience

While individual experiences contribute to the production of ideology, ideologies also contribute to the ways people experience the world. Therefore, at the same time that crimes against Hungarian women provided one way to talk about the nation as a whole, the use of essentialized gender stereotypes to legitimate the idea of the weak nation likewise affected the ways Hungarian women experienced their day-to-day lives. Many members of the Szeged community used the concept of security to frame their personal narratives in 1993–94 and answered the question, "How are you?" with "Tired." Men and women alike spoke of economic insecurities, crime, and the threats to the Hungarian language and nation at the hands of "balkán" foreigners. However, only women were made to feel physically vulnerable and that their right to personal security was taken away from them. It was only women who were told not to walk in Szeged at night or to live alone. It was only women who were made to feel their own bodies were at risk.

Indeed, the experience of women as crime victims was so expected by many in Szeged they found it difficult to speak of men in the same terms. The most personal experience I had with crime in Szeged (which, of course, does not include my time in Serbia) was when a U.S.-American friend's wallet was stolen during a trip to the outdoor market. She was trying to hold several bags of potatoes, cauliflower, carrots, and other food items; her umbrella; and her wallet all at the same time. For just a moment she tucked the wallet into her jacket pocket to rearrange her load and in that instant someone stole it. As I expected, every Hungarian with whom I discussed this event blamed it on a Serb or a foreign Roma. More interesting than this finger-pointing, however, was the comparison between people's reactions to this event and the reaction of a Hungarian acquaintance when her brother's wallet disappeared in the same week. I say "disappeared" rather than stolen because, even though the event was described to me in the same terms I used to describe my friend's experience, my acquaintance was convinced her brother had merely dropped his wallet. It would seem that when a woman lost her wallet in a public space Hungarians automatically assumed she was robbed but when a man had the same experience they assumed he dropped it. She is thought to be a victim of foreign criminals, an object to be acted upon, while he is clumsy and foolish, but an agent who acts rather than one who is acted upon.

As this example begins to illustrate, women in Hungary in the mid-1990s were described and treated as victims, even when suffering the same losses as men. The result of this discourse for many women was that they came to experience the postsocialist world as threatening to their bodies and selves, as well as to their culture, bank accounts, and jobs. Activities in which women formerly participated without giving a thought to their safety, such as tending graves, riding buses, walking home from work, and shopping in the markets, were all experienced as frightening. Only women were glad to live in apartment blocks with paper-thin walls because of the security of knowing the neighbors could hear them scream. From the vantage point of 1994, most women in Szeged looked back fondly on the socialist past as a time of security and relative ease. While men, too, felt the transition from socialism increased their insecurity, I found very few men who agreed with the women that "things were better then."

Kárász utca (street), Szeged.

Gendered Experience, Gendered Nation

I argued in chapter 4 that small-scale agricultural work has been central to Hungarian identities for more than a century. This aspect of the imagined Hungarian community provides another example of the ways in which ideologies of gender and of nation can intersect and inform membership in this community. Hungarian gender ideologies have contributed to a gendered division of agricultural labor in which women and men participate in very different ways. Different gardening tasks provide women and men with access to different kinds of membership in the nation. This difference is not as obvious as the ways in which a militarized national ideology in Israel (Emmett 1996) or the former Yugoslavia (Denich 1995) has allowed for differential access to categories of national belonging for women and men, since, as I stated above, even when women are soldiers, the concept remains masculine. Certainly male soldiers, as they fight for their nation and/or state's sovereignty, experience membership in their nations/states differently than their wives, mothers, and daughters, who belong to the nation through their work as producers and reproducers. The representations of these different kinds of national members will certainly differ as well. However, it is the very invisibility of the workings of gender in national ideologies that often gives them their strength. It is seen as natural in Hungary that women perform some garden tasks and men perform others. That these differences are connected to the ways in which people experience membership in the nation is less obvious.

In my experience with and extensive conversations on gardening in Hungary I found that both women and men in the early and mid-1990s participated in most gardening activities: weeding, watering, planting, and picking. There seemed to be no restrictions for either gender for participation in any of these. However, there was a list of tasks that were very gender specific. Only men took care of fencing, spraying pesticides, taking down large trees, and putting up the house or shed on the plot. While my third landlady could spend hours in her yard, stooped over to pick weeds out of the strawberry patch or stretching up to pick cherries from her trees, she always called her son-in-law to come when it was time to spray for insects. Similarly, as I described in chapter 4, Zoli's wife Éva seemed perfectly able to carry many pounds of fruit and heavy containers of water for long distances, but when it came time to repair a fence, Zoli and a hired hand were left alone to the task. These were clearly gender-specific tasks, as was explained to me when I asked why these women did not do them for themselves, and the gendered division of labor within which my Hungarian acquaintances worked largely excluded women from participating in them.

At the same time, only women in Hungary make jams, syrups, and frozen and preserved fruits and vegetables. While I met many Hungarian men who enjoyed pig slaughtering and outdoor cooking, usually the boiling of a *paprikás* or *pörkölt* (meat stew with onions and paprika that is served over potatoes or dumplings, which are prepared by women), I could find very few men who admitted any knowledge of these other food-related tasks. Zoli occasionally helped Éva run the crusher used to prepare fruit for the making of syrup and jam but even this difficult task, which required at least as much physical strength as spraying pesticides or repairing fences, was seen primarily as women's labor because of its affiliation with food production.

When we examine garden work in Hungary for the gendered ideologies that are built into the division of labor, it becomes evident that men's activities allow the land to become useful. They turn land into useful garden plots through the addition of fences, trees, and, most important, garden houses. As I argued in chapter 4, it is only with the addition of this kind of infrastructure that land becomes useful as a marker of Hungarian identity. Women, on the other hand, deal with the by-products of identity production, fruit and vegetables, which can be composted, thrown out, or otherwise wasted if unneeded, as seen in two of the gardening case studies. While men's activities produce symbolic value, women's activities produce use value. I propose this difference contributes to the imagining of different kinds of national categories and a different kind of investment of the self in the imagined national community.

These gardening differences and their connection to experiencing the nation became even clearer to me through conversations with women and men concerning land and the insecurity of the postsocialist nation. Although these conversations had more to do with agriculture as a whole than about gardening specifically, they do show the ways in which men are more concerned with the symbolic value of land for the nation and women are more concerned with its use value. For example, many more men than women cited the land redistribution program, which in the mid-1990s left much fertile land to lie fallow while its urban owner decided what to do with it, as one of the worst features of the transition from socialism. When I asked why this was so important, most men cited the loss of agricultural autonomy and need for importing foreign grain. Foreign grain, for the people of a nation that has identified itself as a food exporter for decades, is a clear symbol of insecurity. While women are also concerned about productive land and foreign grain, their concern lies much more in the result of these haphazard policies: the rise in bread prices. Many women and almost no men cited the cost of bread as the best example of the insecurity of the Hungarian nation in the postsocialist era. Therefore, while both Hungarian women and men in Szeged characterize their nation as insecure, the route through which each arrived at this conclusion was very different. At least in part, these different conclusions are connected to gender ideologies as they are played out in the division of garden labor.

Another way to approach this intersection of gender and national ideologies is to look at people's networks and relationships through a gendered lens. I argued in chapter 3 that one way individuals imagine the national community is through their own experiences in local communities and networks. Certainly in Hungary, as everywhere, personal relationships between friends, acquaintances, colleagues, neighbors, and family are informed by gender differences. In Hungary, these differences begin with parental expectations for sons and daughters.

Despite the fact that Hungarian women made some strides toward gender equity in educational opportunity and employment during the socialist era, if only in terms of numbers rather than status and wage scales (Kulcsár 1985), parental expectations continue in the postsocialist era to be for sons to find good jobs and for daughters to find good husbands. Girls are expected to stay close to home and, indeed, to desire this, while boys are freer to go out into the world (Jávor 1990). I was told these things by many people, both old and young, male and female, and I myself faced a barrage of questions, especially from older women, about why I, as a "girl" (as an unmarried woman, I was referred to as "little girl" for my entire time in Szeged), would want to live so far from my parents' home. Another question I faced regularly concerned my finding a nice Hungarian man, marrying him, and moving to Szeged forever. Most people assumed that as a twenty-six-year-old woman I was actively looking for a husband and would gladly have married a Hungarian man if I had the opportunity. Few believed my vociferous denials of such expectations or hopes for my year and a half in Hungary (see Huseby-Darvas 1987:15-16).

For Hungarian girls and young women, parental expectations and the resulting restrictions on activity often (but not always) mean different access to group membership and possibilities for making and keeping networks than their brothers. For example, a twenty-year-old female acquaintance of mine, Erzsébet, told me this story of her brief membership in a Christian community group in Szeged. Her sister had joined the group first, in 1991, and Erzsébet began accompanying her to the twice-weekly meetings early in 1992. After several months she became quite attached to the group, both because it was answering some of her questions about God, religion, and spirituality, and because it provided her with a network of people upon whom she could rely, if only in the area of spiritual questioning. By late spring 1992, however, she began to see a change in their mother, with whom she and her brother and sister lived. Their mother warned the two young women continuously of the dangers of these kinds of religious cults. She verbalized her resentment of the time they spent away from home. If they decided to study the Bible rather than join their mother watching television she would interrupt, nitpick, and undermine their beliefs. In the end, Erzsébet decided to stop attending the group rather than make waves at home. She was very sad at having to give up access to the knowledge of the group's leaders and possibility for further spiritual growth, but felt it was wrong and against Christ's teachings to leave her mother home alone so much. She did not cite the loss of community or acquaintances as one of the reasons for her sadness.

Erzsébet's sister continued to attend the meetings, however, and became engaged to a fellow member soon after her sister quit. Their mother would not agree to hold the engagement party, through which engagements are publicly recognized in Hungary, until the man had been working at his job for six months. She claimed that she did not want her daughter to marry someone who has no salary, which seemed somewhat reasonable to me given the state of the Hungarian economy at the time. Erzsébet was convinced, however, that the real reason for the forced delay was her mother's desire to keep the couple apart and her sister at home for as long as possible. She explained that their mother wasn't against the marriage, but she did not want to give up sole access to her daughter's domestic labor. Although marriage is the final goal of many mothers for their daughters in Szeged, there is a conflicting desire to keep female children at home to contribute to the domestic economy and workload.

While Erzsébet and her sister were both affected by their mother's desire to keep them around the house after work and in the evenings, their brother was allowed to lead a very different kind of life. He was a member of two different sports teams and spent a great deal of time and money in the pursuit of these activities. He traveled abroad several times per year to play in international tournaments, traveled within Hungary many weekends, and spent most evenings at team practices. Their mother never tried to limit his access to his clubs and teams and even helped him pay the entrance fees and traveling expenses required of him to remain on these teams. When it would interfere with his sporting activities he was not required to help at home and in general his domestic chores were minimal in comparison with his sisters'. When I asked both Erzsébet and her brother about the double standard they said it is different for boys and girls in Hungary. Boys are supposed to go out and make contacts that may help them later; girls are expected to stay home, help their mothers, and learn how to care for a home and family.

A second example of the kinds of pressure exerted on women to limit their personal networks comes from an older, retired woman from Sopron, a bustling tourist town on the Austrian border in northwest Hungary, whom I met while she was visiting her sister's family in Szeged. Mrs. Feher was the only Hungarian I met in Szeged who spoke of friends and friendships positively. She said she has so many friends in Sopron, if she visited one each day she would be busy all week long and still not have seen everyone. She criticized her Szeged relatives for all the time they spent working, both for the extra hours they spent at their jobs and the time they put in at their garden. She enjoyed the freedom to visit her friends, go to the theater, or travel with them; she also visited her more distant relatives who live in various cities and towns throughout Hungary. According to statements from both this woman and her sister's husband, she was no more financially secure than most other widowed, retired women in Hungary, but, as she said herself, she did not allow the insecurities of the mid-1990s to cut into her circle of friends and family. These ties had always been important to her and she wasn't going to change just because the political system in Hungary had changed. However, her sister seemed to resent these ties and tried to keep her in Szeged working with them throughout the summer of 1993.

When I first met Mrs. Feher in June 1993, her summer plans were to spend a couple of weeks in Szeged, another week in Kecskemét (a city one hour north of Szeged) with a cousin, two weeks at Lake Balaton with her neighbor, and to attend the wedding of a distant relative of her husband's, with whose parents she has maintained contact for decades, in Austria. She wound up remaining in Szeged for more than six weeks that summer, because every time she began making plans to leave her sister told her they needed her help. One time they decided it was time to make brandy; a second opportunity to leave came up and she was asked to stay until the cherries were all processed into syrup. She had to cut the trip to Kecskemét entirely and did not have any opportunity to get anything done at home between returning from Szeged and going to Lake Balaton.

Like Erzsébet, Mrs. Feher felt guilty about leaving her sister when she and her husband obviously did not want her to go. She was frustrated at her inability to finish her travel plans and do some summer chores at home, but she was also glad to be able to help. Her own domestic tasks to maintain a small apartment just for herself in Sopron were minimal, she said, and she liked being able occasionally "to work like a woman again." As these two examples help to illustrate, playing on people's sense of duty or obligation was an important social control mechanism for family members to coerce others into limiting their networks and connections outside of their immediate family circle. This is particularly true for women who tried to leave the confines of domestic labor for a more expansive world of acquaintances and extended kin.

I found in both my time-use survey and discussions with women and men that neither had any more friends than the other; women and men equally answered the question, "Do you have friends?" in the negative. However, many men did have more access to acquaintances and contacts outside the immediate family circle than many women, particularly younger women with children. The woman I described in chapter 3 who spends her time with "nobody" and whose husband has lost contact with his friends from high school is a good example of these gender differences. As I said before, in 1993–94 this woman was home on child-care leave with her two small children while her husband worked a variety of jobs to support their family. She was envious of her husband's circle of acquaintances and the number of adults he saw and spoke with during the course of his day as a salesman. He claimed to have no time to maintain his friendships from the past and spoke of an inability to engage with people, yet at the same time he met new people on a daily basis and spent his entire working day in social situations. His wife spent her time alone with two small children. These two people spoke of their networks in the same terms but their actual situations differed tremendously due to the assumption in Hungary that it is women who stay at home and care for young children.

The same can also be said of couples in which both the husband and wife work outside the home. In most cases, women leave their place of employment to come home and begin three or more hours of domestic labor. Even among young couples, the new wife is the one who does most of the cooking, cleaning, shopping, and other household work; this is true even in cases where the woman claims no prior ability or desire to cook or works more hours outside the home than her husband. Freedom from these tasks leaves men more time to work a second job, often obtained through acquaintances or relatives; to join organizations such as sports teams, religious groups, or work circles; and to maintain a network of colleagues and acquaintances, if not friends, that are much more difficult for women to find and preserve.

Both women and men in Szeged said in 1993-94 that they had no time for people outside of their immediate family circle, they were disappointed in people they thought were friends, and it was as dangerous to allow strangers into their networks as it was to allow them into their courtyards and homes. The end result, however, is that many girls stay home while their brothers go out and join clubs and teams. Some women spend their days alone with just their children to speak with, others come home from a long day at work to take care of the household work alone while their husbands spend these hours with colleagues or acquaintances. Still other women are widowed and left either alone or to care for their mothers or grandchildren. The experiences through which women and men are able to imagine the more distant and abstract national community differ tremendously.

Despite all this ethnographic data pointing to different kinds of masculine and feminine members of the Hungarian nation, it would not be accurate to conclude that women and men have different imagined national communities. Both women and men in Hungary share a set of ideas about what it means to be gendered members of the national community. Hungarian men cannot experience what it means to be a Hungarian woman, nor vice versa, but they can and do understand the world through the same set of gendered national ideologies. Both women and men use crimes against women to symbolize crimes against the feminized nation; the ideologies are the same while the experience and representation differ. This is as true of Hungary as of all national communities.

Official Discourse

At the same time that many of my acquaintances in Szeged were talking about crimes against women and the dangers for women of walking alone on the streets, more elite and politically powerful Hungarians were likewise drawing upon naturalized gender images to represent certain issues and ideas to the Hungarian people. During the national elections in May 1994, numerous political parties employed specific gendered images to represent themselves as either the most Hungarian choice for the second free electoral period, the most secure, or both. For example, SzDSz featured their candidate for prime minister and his wife on numerous posters that hung in Szeged. One poster featuring this couple shows them walking down the street arm in arm; the text states, "I chose him fifteen years ago." The implication is that because the candidate is a stable and loyal husband and cares well for his wife and family, he will be a stable and loyal prime minister and care well for the nation and state. Like his wife, voters will be satisfied over the long term that he is their best choice. Another image chosen by this party is of the candidate and an older woman standing on a street corner. The woman is holding a locally made wicker shopping basket; the candidate is standing very near to her, with his head turned to look at and perhaps speak with the woman. The text states, "She trusts in him." The image of the shopping basket indicates this woman is out in Szeged for the purpose of fulfilling her duty to care for her home and family. Perhaps the text indicates she trusts in the candidate to improve Hungary's economy and thus allow her to continue feeding her family. Or, perhaps she trusts in him to protect her from the foreign pickpockets and swindlers many Hungarians believe spend their days in Szeged's public markets. Either way, the image relies upon taken-for-granted Hungarian gender roles for efficacy in attracting voters.

The Independent Smallholders' Party likewise employed gendered imagery in their campaign posters in Szeged prior to the May 1994 elections. This party's most common poster, in Szeged anyway, was even more explicit than SzDSz's in its use of familiar gender images. The picture on their poster is of a woman holding a very young infant in her arms; the text reads: "If you don't have children/family, you don't have a home/nation. If you don't have morals, you don't have a nation." The text and image are promoting both a pronatalist and a pronationalist ideology and in doing so depict the ideal Hungarian woman as the mother in both her own home and her homeland.

Outside of organized political parties, academics and journalists also are considered elite in Hungary, at least to the degree that they are considered experts and reliable sources of information. In their own ways, some of the members of these categories also have contributed gendered representations of the Hungarian nation and its members to the general discourse on identities in the postsocialist era. One common image from the earliest years of the transition, though it began as early as the early 1980s (Goven 1993), is of Hungarian women as the pawns of the communists in their attempts to destroy the nation. Enikő Bollobás, an academic and political figure from Szeged, has published an essay in English in which she echoes statements made by other academics, journalists, and politicians on this topic. She says, "Women were used by those in power" (1993:202).

This statement is a much less combative version of the discourse political scientist Joanna Goven cites in her essay on gender politics in Hungary (1993). She uses quotations from Hungarian sociologist Miklós Hernádi, former secretary of education Kata Beke, and journalist Magda Gubi, among others, to show how in Hungary many believe the offenses of the Socialist Workers' Party against the nation were as much about gender as they were about the nation. For example, Gubi writes, socialist "society liberates the woman from family shackles, gives her economic independence, spares her many of the burdens of childrearing, and in exchange asks for an alliance in crushing male obstinacy" (cited in Goven 1993:232). Other examples of this kind of discourse are even more explicit in making connections between powerful women and the party. Hernádi sees women's emancipation, along with divorce laws and laws that favor mothers in custody cases, as destroying Hungarian society (Goven 1993). For Beke, as well, any change in "traditional" Hungarian gender inequalities is deemed dangerous for society as a whole; "this gender bipolarity is critical to the health and well-being of society" (Goven 1993:229).

Like the individuals with whom I spoke in Hungary, these political, academic, and cultural figures use naturalized, taken-for-granted, gender images and ideologies as tools in their constructions of other identities. These affective images are effective in this context because, as a whole, Hungarians generally share ideas about masculinity and femininity. These constructs serve as a common base upon which it is possible to naturalize other ideologies and identities. These ideologies are, of course, historically contingent and ever-changing in content. Yet, even just a brief look into Hungarian history is enough to illustrate that gendered images were used politically in Hungary in every period in the twentieth century and women in Hungary were often discursively aligned with threats to the national community.

Gender and the Death of the Nation

The period of my fieldwork in Hungary was not much different than other periods in the twentieth century for the ways in which Hungarians were concerned about "the imminent death of the nation" (Gal 1994:269), and for their use of familiar gender constructs to legitimate this concern. For example, anthropologist Éva Huseby-Darvas cites references to Hungary in the 1920s, or the post-Trianon period, as "the white and virginal, but mutilated and bleeding, body of the beloved motherland" and "the revered body of the motherland, torn asunder and ravaged by barbarians" (1996:169). These images represent the Hungarian nation as a woman crime victim, suffering at the hands of Hungary's "balkán" neighbors. The use of rape as a figure of speech in nationalist literature and discourse is very common to represent the weakened nation (Enloe 1995). Either the nation itself is represented as a raped woman, as in this example, or the women of the nation are represented as rape victims or potential victims, as in the example of the Hungarian woman and the Serbian border guard. In both cases, what is being represented is a feminine nation with masculine enemies. As is obvious from these examples, both representations were used in Hungary in the twentieth century.

At the same time the nation was being represented as a feminized victim in the post-Trianon period, its female members were being represented very differently. Rather than as victims of outside aggression, Hungarian women were often represented as powerful threats from within. The nation was seen to be at demographic risk, largely because of the "danger of rural 'matriarchy'—(old) women exercising too much power in the countryside" (Gal 1994:270). What this statement refers to is Populist writers' fears in the 1930s that Hungary's low birth rate was contributing to a slow death of the nation, begun at Trianon. What was particularly odious to these authors was the Hungarian "one child system," in which Hungarian peasants effectively limited their families to one child in order to prevent the division of small family land holdings (Gal 1994:269–70; Vasary 1989). Rural women were being blamed in this discourse for nothing less than collaborating with the authors of the Trianon peace settlement to kill the nation, while Hungarian men remained free of any taint at all.

Although Trianon has remained an important symbol of the threat to the Hungarian nation posed by its neighbors and of Hungary's tragic past, during the socialist era it was no longer seen as the most immediate and pressing threat to the nation. During this era, the Communist Party (which became the Hungarian Socialist Workers' Party following the 1956 revolution) and socialist system replaced Trianon and hostile neighbors as the primary threats to the national community. At the same time, despite the new external enemy, women were once again linked to this primary threat to the nation. "Women [were] portrayed not as victims of a state-sponsored 'emancipation' that overburdened them but rather as powerful agents who . . . responded to state emancipation by becoming destructive to men and children" (Goven 1993:225). As Susan Gal argues with regard to the abortion debate during the first year or two of the transition, "In much of this material an implicit equation is drawn between women allied with the former Communist state, as against men who are linked to a new, law-governed state and society" (1994:276; Huseby-Darvas 1996). In both cases, women are represented as dangerous to men, children, and the nation. As in the post-Trianon period, women were represented as collaborators with the enemy; men and the nation were their victims.

In the early postsocialist period, Hungarians once again feared for their nation at the hands of foreign enemies. Rather than nostalgia, the perception of similar structural and material relations between Hungary and her neighbors precipitated similar reactions of fear. In the post-World War I period military, ideological, and territorial loss; radical system change; and foreign invasion all resulted in great fear for the security and continuity of the Hungarian nation. The transition from socialism in Hungary created a political climate in the mid-1990s that many Hungarians saw as similar to the one in which Hungary found itself between 1918 and 1922. Many Hungarians with whom I spoke of the past connected or compared the mid-1990s with the immediate post-Trianon period. In response to these perceived similarities in structural and material relations, Hungarians reacted in similar ways, by fearing for the security and continuity of the Hungarian nation. One of the most commonly used metaphors for addressing these insecurities was crime, specifically, crimes against women. In the early and mid-1990s, women in Hungary were seen as weak, vulnerable, and at risk of crime by foreigners; they were no longer represented as the "powerful agents" of the antifeminist discourse in the late socialist and early postsocialist periods (Goven 1993:225). At the same time, women continued to be associated with threats to the nation. Since the threat changed, however, the representation of women likewise changed to maintain the equation between women and threats to national continuity.

Throughout the twentieth century Hungarians constructed discursive links between women and that which they found threatening to the continuation of the nation. Representations of women were used by both women and men in gendered political discourse to talk about the enemy of their nation. At the same time, Hungarians also represented the nation itself as a gendered individual. These representations made sense in this context because Hungarians in general share ideas about what it means to be a woman, what it means to be a man, and how the two genders should interact with each other. These are experienced as a natural part of day-to-day life.

Conclusion

Participation in and the experience of all the local practices that allow people to imagine the nation are constrained and circumscribed by gender. In Hungary this was as true in the mid-1990s as it was during the socialist era when competing ideologies of work were what defined the nation, as during the interwar period when loss of territory and irredentism defined the nation, and as during the pre-World War I period when agricultural work and peasant values defined the nation. In addition, in each of these eras, Hungarians used gender to construct and naturalize ideologies of the nation. The end result of these processes of legitimation is that the nation becomes imbued with the same gendered norms and values as the communities that imagined it into being in the first place.

Furthermore, the Hungarian case is not unique, either for its use of gender or for its relegation of women to an inferior position in the nation. At the same time, mere recognition that national cultures subordinate women does not tell us anything new. Feminists have long known we have yet to find a society in which women and men are represented equally in ideology or symbol, or in which they are equal in social structural relations (Ortner 1974). The goal, then, is to ask for each nation what local-level experiences have contributed to the production of national ideologies and how gender constrains and enables these experiences.

CHAPTER 8

Conclusion

Hungarian sociologist Zsuzsa Ferge's conjecture that the exchange of existential security for freedom as defined in the West will be largely negative for many Hungarians (1991:132) became reality by the early and mid-1990s. No one knew what each day would bring. One day you have a job and an apartment and you can buy bread, the next day you may have lost everything. As one life-long resident of Szeged expressed in 1994, "You used to wake up and know exactly how things are. Now things change daily. You never know what will happen next." Interconnected with this existential insecurity in material terms was a concomitant increase in existential insecurity in philosophical terms. This interconnection is dramatically evident in the reduction of the strength and breadth of personal networks and the pervasive discourses on crime, foreigners, borders, and the body; on being tired and fad vitamins; on hoarding and provisioning; and on the criminal threats to Hungarians by "balkán" foreigners. While most Hungarians did not desire a complete return to the previous political and economic system, they were not prepared for the anxieties that seemed to accompany freedom from state paternalism. As a result, it was impossible to speak with a Hungarian in Szeged in 1993–94 and not be forced to confront the existential security issues (both material and philosophical) they said faced them as individuals and as members of their local communities.

At the same time that my Hungarian acquaintances spoke of the insecurities they were experiencing as individuals and local community members, they were also using these experiences to talk about a larger, more abstract community to which they feel they belong: the Hungarian nation. Their experiences in their local communities provided some of the constructs through which they made sense of the national experience with the political and economic processes of the transition. Each time they heard of a robbery in their own city, purchased bread at prices twenty times higher than in the 1980s, or began working a second or third job in order to pay the rent, these

135

Hungarians imagined that this also was the experience of others who for historical, linguistic, cultural, and political reasons consider themselves and are considered by others to be Hungarian.

As I have tried to express throughout this book, I believe that this Hungarian identification of the person, community, and nation as insecure is the result of the actual social and material relations of the transition from socialism. There is no doubt that the cost of living in Hungary increased dramatically in the early 1990s without a significant increase in wages, crime rates increased, and unemployment rates were higher than they had been for decades. In 1994, unemployment was at 10.4% (www.ems.psu.edu), inflation was at 22.5% (users.ox.ac.uk), the currency was devalued for the fifth time in almost as many years, and Hungary's foreign debt was still the largest per capita in the region (cited in Van Hoorn, et al. 2000:70). Existential security, in material terms, did decrease for a large number of Hungarians.

At the same time, I argue that the particular construction of insecurity that emerged in Szeged at this time, which included both material and philosophical aspects, is both culturally and historically contingent. Being a Hungarian living in Szeged in the mid-1990s meant bringing a large number of "lenses" to bear in interpreting this quantifiable decrease in material security. For example, both "pre-socialist traditions and legacies" and "the 40 year legacy of socialist political economy [and] interpersonal suspicions" (Sampson 1991:19) affected Hungarians' interpretations of their situations. Similarly, both ideas about what it means to be Hungarian generally and ideas about what it means to reside in Szeged specifically also affected these particular Hungarians' perceptions of their lives.

In addition, the meanings of such concepts as "balkán," "Europe," gardens, friends, family, women, and many others discussed in this book are not separable from their cultural and historic backgrounds in Szeged. These ideas were important markers of insecurity not because they are inherently tied to this idea, but because of the ways many people in this city perceived them as being so. For example, a different community, with a different history, culture, and self-identity, might have reacted to the actual contraction of the economy by expanding their kin and friend networks to draw upon the resources of a larger community, rather than constricting them. A different community might have reacted very positively to the influx of foreign shoppers in their city because of the increased revenue from their business, rather than seeing them as criminals. A different community might have spoken of gardening in very negative terms because of its connotations, rather than seeing it as a way out of insecurity. A different community might have seen men as a more salient symbol of insecurity than women because of their association with politics, economics, and criminality. And so on. Therefore, while none of these reactions are unique to Szeged, for example, using foreigners as scapegoats in difficult economic times is extremely common, they are also not necessarily generalizable to other postsocialist communities. It is only through the holism of the ethnographic project that we are able to speak about the different ways structure and process, experience and perception, history and ideology all come together to create each community's unique understanding of who they are and what defines them.

Epilogue: Return

I returned to Szeged in July 1996 after two years away from Hungary. At this point I had already finished my dissertation on the research I had gathered in 1993–94 on security and the nation and was going back to explore a different topic, the celebrations of the 1100-year anniversary of the nation. I knew I would be returning to Szeged a very changed person and I expected my friends and acquaintances likewise to have changed somewhat. Yet I was still unprepared for some of the difficulties I faced on this return trip after a mere two years away. I was also unprepared for some of the unexpected joys I had during those eight weeks.

My arrival in 1996 was vastly different from my stressful entry into fieldwork in January 1993. This time I flew into Budapest's Ferihegy Airport and was able to speak at length with the customs and immigration officials in their language. I was able to ignore the offers of taxicab rides I received from both official and unofficial drivers as I looked for one of my friends, who had driven all the way from Szeged to meet my plane. I recognized the familiar land and settlement patterns of the Alföld on the three-hour drive back to Szeged. I spoke constantly, and in complete sentences, with my friend during the drive south. Rather than being dropped at a prostitute motel far from the city center, my friend insisted I come home with him and spend as much time as I like with him and his wife.

Indeed, many of my experiences in those first few days back in Hungary surprised me because they were as comforting and secure as a homecoming. The same people who claimed rather vociferously two years before that I was not their friend greeted me with big hugs, kisses, and, in one case, even tears of joy. I had to promise to set aside several weekend meals, including my birthday, to share with Zoli and Éva. Viki and her husband had me to their apartment for drinks and later invited me to meet them for dinner at one of Szeged's many pizzerias. One of my acquaintances who lives in a village outside of Szeged was very disappointed to learn I couldn't afford the time away from my research in Szeged and Budapest to spend a long weekend with him. Everybody I visited in Szeged made me feel more welcome and assured my feelings of friendship were reciprocated more than I ever felt during my previous time in Hungary.

However, I soon found that despite the security of my welcome, the intervening two years had changed both me and my Szeged friends and acquaintances significantly. In the two years I was away, I had written and defended my doctoral dissertation, moved across the country, and began teaching full time. Whereas I had arrived in Hungary the first time as a graduate student, living on very limited funds and somewhat insecure about my credentials as a researcher, I was returning as a fully employed professional. I carried business cards with my title and degrees on them to legitimate both my presence in the country and my research project. Even more important, I arrived knowing where my next paycheck was coming from and that it would be enough to cover my expenses both during my time in Hungary and at home. Although my acquaintances still insisted upon calling me "the little girl," I knew I had come back to Szeged as an adult, and I suspect many of them knew this as well.

Like me, who looked much the same as I had two years earlier but had changed in significant ways, Szeged too appeared much the same but was a very different place. Certainly, there were quite a large number of new shops on the main route between Budapest and Szeged, a local pizzeria had been replaced by a Pizza Hut franchise, a distant relative of the murdered pastry chef had reopened the shop, and many older buildings were in the process of either being replaced or receiving substantial facelifts. Nevertheless, these changes were minor and relatively insignificant. Szeged was still Szeged; the fountain was still its heart, the people walking in the pedestrian center of town were still its soul.

Unfortunately, this soul had undergone changes that were not visible in the city's external presentation. Nearly everyone I visited and spoke with during the summer of 1996 was deeply disappointed with life in the transition. I had certainly come up against what Hungarians almost proudly refer to as their "national pessimism" during my earlier fieldwork, but this seemed quite

The heart of Szeged.

different. Even my most optimistic acquaintances from my first fieldwork period, successful small business owners, cheerful artists, and satisfied pensioners, spoke with a very different voice in 1996 than they had two years earlier. One acquaintance told me of her daughter's suicide attempt due to family problems related to her husband's business failure. Most people complained of rising prices without any concomitant rise in salaries. My acquaintances who had supported the election of the Socialist Party in May 1994 and had begun that summer with high hopes for increased government responsibility and attention to Hungary's economic woes seemed to have resigned themselves to Hungary's economic failure and the inability of any political solution to improve their lives. The epithet "Wild East" was even more frequently employed to refer to Hungary than it had been in 1993–94. If the Hungarian nation and its members were insecure in 1993–94, many were also hopeful the processes of transition were eventually going to make their and their children's lives better. At that time, they and their nation were insecure, but there was hope for the future. In 1996, not only had the insecurities increased, but the hope for a better life was diminished. Most people I know in Szeged felt they were more insecure in 1996 than they had been at any time before.

Obviously, the contrast between my life and those of my Hungarian friends and acquaintances was, for the most part, even greater than it had once been. I arrived back in Szeged more secure than I had ever been. Financially, I did not have to concern myself with rising prices or budget shopping. During my first fieldwork period, I, like many Hungarians, had to limit my spending to live within my budget. Even considering the strength of the U.S. dollar, which almost always kept up with Hungary's inflation rate during my first stay, I still had to spend time going to different stores and markets to be able to spend fewer forints on bread, rice, pasta, and vegetables. During my second trip, however, I was in Szeged for a short amount of time and, while my grant money from the University of the Pacific was not completely unlimited, I was never concerned about overspending. I noticed it took far more forints to feed myself than it had two years earlier but was uncomfortable talking about this with my acquaintances. For me, the increase meant very little in relation to my professor's salary and research grant, whereas for them it was becoming more and more difficult to survive on their monthly wages.

I was also much more secure about my future in the summer of 1996 than I had been two years before. Even having completed my fieldwork, in 1994 I was not secure in the knowledge I would complete my dissertation to the satisfaction of my committee or, if I did, that I would get a full-time teaching position. Two years later, I had reached both goals and was looking ahead positively towards the next set of goals. Conversely, many of my Hungarian friends and acquaintances had been very sure in 1994 that life in Hungary generally, and their lives specifically, would improve with the election of MSzP in May 1994. In the summer of 1996, however, not only had the situation not improved, but for many people existential security was even more tenuous than it had been.

I enjoyed my eight weeks in Szeged in 1996 but, because of these contrasts, it was also a difficult time for me in ways I did not expect. Listening to people talk about their financial, family, or other problems was more difficult than it had ever been previously. Having to accept their resignation that the transition from socialism was not going to improve Hungarians' lives for another generation or more was more painful than it had been earlier. Certainly, I had not enjoyed listening to these kinds of discourses in the past, but because I, too, was insecure in so many ways and had come to share my Hungarian acquaintances' view of their world as insecure, they had seemed almost natural. When I returned in 1996 with a completely different outlook, the contrasts between our life situations seemed vast. Indeed, if it were not for this return trip, I might have become concerned that my own insecurities during 1993–94 had caused me to overstate my informants' feelings and experiences; having gone back and listened to their concerns, I am assured this is not the case.

I do not know the degree to which my Hungarian friends and acquaintances felt the differences between our situations in 1996. What I do know is that I am glad in 1993–94 I was able to share in the lives of some Hungarians and begin to understand how they see themselves in the world. Even if I am never able to go back to Hungary for such a long period of time, or am never able to share in my Hungarian friends' and acquaintances' experiences to the degree I did during that first research period, I am grateful that they shared with me their disappointment in the transition from socialism and their views about what it means to be a member of the Hungarian nation in the postsocialist world. Going back to Szeged in 1996, while personally difficult, served to reinforce in my mind that the arguments I make throughout this book concerning the importance of insecurity in the construction of a postsocialist Hungarian identity are representative of the imaginings of many Hungarians during the mid-1990s.

Bibliography

Anderson, Benedict. 1983. Imagined Communities. London: Verso.

Barany, George. 1969. Hungary: From Aristocratic to Proletarian Nationalism. In Nationalism in Eastern Europe. Peter F. Sugar and Ivo J. Lederer, eds. pp. 259–309. Seattle: University of Washington Press.

Bell, Peter D. 1984. Peasants in Socialist Transition. Berkeley: University of California Press.

Benz, Stephen Connely. 1996. Guatemalan Journey. Austin: University of Texas Press.

Berend, Iván T. 1990. Contemporary Hungary 1956–1984. In A History of Hungary. Peter F. Sugar, ed. pp. 384–404. Bloomington: Indiana University Press.

Bernstein, Ken. 1990. Berlitz Blueprint Hungary. Lausanne, Switzerland: Berlitz Publishing.

Bollobás, Enikő. 1993. "Totalitarian Lib": The Legacy of Communism for Hungarian Women. In Gender Politics and Post-Communism. Nanette Funk and Magda Mueller, eds. pp. 201–6. New York: Routledge.

Bruszt, László and David Stark. 1991. Remaking the Political Field in Hungary: From the Politics of Confrontation to the Politics of Competition. Journal of International Affairs 45(1):201–45.

Burawoy, Michael. 1988. Piece Rates, Hungarian Style. In On Work. R. E. Pahl, ed. pp. 210–28. New York: Basil Blackwell.

Cohen, Anthony P. Personal Nationalism: A Scottish View of Some Rites, Rights and Wrongs. American Ethnologist 23(4):1–14.

———. 2000. Peripheral Vision: Nationalism, National Identity and the Objective Correlative in Scotland. In Signifying Identities. Anthony P. Cohen, ed. pp. 145–69. New York: Routledge.

Corrin, Chris. 1994. Magyar Women. New York: St. Martin's Press.

Creed, Gerald W. 1998. Domesticating Revolution. University Park: University of Pennsylvania Press.

Csepeli, György. 1989. Structures and Contents of Hungarian National Identity. English text by Chris Tennant. New York: Verlag Peter Lang.

Csepeli, György and Antal Örkeny. 1992. From Unjust Equality to Just Inequality. The New Hungarian Quarterly 33:71–76.

Cushing, G. F. 1960. The Birth of National Literature in Hungary. Slavonic and East European Review 38(91):459–75.

Délmagyarország. 1994. January 26A:7. Négyes gyilkosság a Bárka utcában (Four Murders on Bárka Street).

———. 1994. January 26B:7. Beszélgetés dr. Dornbach Alajossal, a Parlament alelnökével (Conversation with Dr. Alajos Dornbach, Vice President of Parliament).

———. 1994. January 27A:7. A városi rendőrkapitány és tanácsnok a közbiztonságrol: Egyedi eset az alvilág számláján (The City Police and Councilmen on Public Security: Individual Instances on the Bill of the Underworld).

———. 1994. January 27B:7. Hány sakál bérelhető néhány órára? (How Many Jackals Can Be Rented For a Few Hours?).

———. 1994. January 27C:7. A Hét Kérdése: Elszabadul a pokol? (Question of the Week: Has All Hell Broken Loose?).

———. 1994. January 28A:7. A polgármester a rendőrség megerősítését szorgalmazza (The Mayor Presses for Reinforcement).

———. 1994. January 28B:7. Mi is tiltakozunk! (We Also Protest!).

———. 1994. February 2:16. Csendes demonstráció (Quiet Demonstration).

———. 1994. February 4:1,3. Ötszáz bizony csöndesen ment (At Least Five Hundred Went Quietly). (Szegedi spelling in original).

———. 1994. February 10:4. A Hét Kérdése: Félnünk kell a városban? (Question of the Week: Do We Need to Fear in the City?).

———. 1994. February 11:7. Gazdaság és félelem (Economy and Fear).

———. 1994. February 17:6. Stresszben hamarabb elsül a fegyver (The Weapon Fires Sooner in Stress).

———. 1994. February 24:4. A Hét Kérdése: Nem unja még a vérfürdőt? (Question of the Week: Aren't You Afraid of the Bloodbath?).

———. 1994. February 26:15. Csongrád megyéről, Szegedről, a közbiztonságrol (1). Állandósulnak-e az indulatok? (About Csongrád County, About Szeged, About Their Public Security (1). Have Dispositions Become Stable?).

———. 1994. March 1:11. Csongrád megyéről, Szegedről, a közbiztonságrol (3). Bűnös város-e Szeged? (About Csongrád County, About Szeged, About Their Public Security (3). Is Szeged a City of Crime?).

———. 1994. March 3:13. Csongrád megyéről, Szegedről, a közbiztonságrol (5). Bűnözés, biztonság és demokrácia (About Csongrád County, About Szeged, About Their Public Security (5). Crime, Security and Democracy).

———. 1994. March 4:17. Mit mond a statisztika? "Bűnös" városok, megyék (What Do the Statistics Say? "Crime" Cities, Counties).

———. 1994. May 7:3. Jönnek a jugoszlávok, mennek a magyarok (The Yugoslavs Come, the Hungarians Go).

Denich, Bette. 1995. Of Arms, Men, and Ethnic War in (Former) Yugoslavia. In Feminism, Nationalism, and Militarism. Connie Sutton, ed. pp. 61–71. Washington, DC: Association for Feminist Anthropology.

Douglas, Mary. 1972. Deciphering a Meal. Daedalus 101(winter, 1):61–81.

Emmett, Ayala. 1996. Our Sisters' Promised Land: Women, Politics, and Israeli-Palestinian Coexistence. Ann Arbor: University of Michigan Press.

Enloe, Cynthia. 1995. Feminism, Nationalism and Militarism: Wariness Without Paralysis? In Feminism, Nationalism, and Militarism. Connie Sutton, ed. pp. 13–32. Washington, DC: Association for Feminist Anthropology.

Fehér, Ferenc. 1982. Paternalism as a Mode of Legitimation in Soviet-type Societies. *In* Political Legitimation in Communist States. T. H. Rigby and Ferenc Fehér, eds., pp. 64–81. New York: St. Martin's Press.

Fél, Edit and Tamás Hofer. 1969. Proper Peasants: Traditional Life in a Hungarian Village. New York: Wenner-Gren Foundation for Anthropological Research.

Ferge, Zsuzsa. 1979. A Society in the Making. White Plains, NY: M. E. Sharpe, Inc.

———. 1991. Recent Trends in Social Policy in Hungary. *In* Economic Reforms and Welfare Systems in the USSR, Poland and Hungary. Jan Adam, ed. pp. 132–55. New York: St. Martin's Press.

Foster, Robert. 1991. Making National Cultures in the Global Ecumene. Annual Review of Anthropology 20:235–60.

Fox, Richard G. 1990. Introduction. *In* Nationalist Ideologies and the Production of National Cultures, Richard G. Fox, ed. pp. 1–14. American Ethnological Society Monograph Series Number 2. Washington, D.C.: American Anthropological Association.

Gagnon, Jr., V. P. 1991. Yugoslavia: Prospects for Stability. Foreign Affairs 70(3):17–35.

Gal, Susan. 1991. Bartók's Funeral: Representations of Europe in Hungarian Political Rhetoric. American Ethnologist 18(3):440–58.

———. 1994. Gender in the Post-Socialist Transition: The Abortion Debate in Hungary. East European Politics and Societies 8(2):256–85.

Geertz, Clifford. 1973. The Interpretation of Cultures. New York: Basic Books.

Glatz, Ferenc. 1983. Backwardness, Nationalism, Historiography. East European Quarterly 27(1):31–40.

Goven, Joanna. 1993. Gender Politics in Hungary: Autonomy and Antifeminism. *In* Gender Politics and Post-Communism. Nanette Funk and Magda Mueller, eds. pp. 224–40. New York: Routledge.

György, Andrew. 1966. The Role of Nationalism in Eastern Europe: From Monolith to Polycentrism. *In* Eastern Europe in Transition. Kurt London, ed. pp. 3–18. Baltimore: Johns Hopkins Press.

Handler, Richard. 1988. Nationalism and the Politics of Culture in Quebec. Madison: University of Wisconsin Press.

Heller, Agnes. 1982. Phases of Legitimation in Soviet-type Societies. *In* Political Legitimation in Communist States. T. H. Rigby and Ferenc Fehér, eds. pp. 45–63. New York: St. Martin's Press.

Helmreich, Ernst Christian, ed. 1957. Hungary. New York: Praeger.

Hoensch, Jörg K. 1988. A History of Modern Hungary 1867–1986. London: Longman Group. Translated by Kim Traynor.

Hofer, Tamás. 1991. Construction of the 'Folk Cultural Heritage' in Hungary and Rival Versions of National Identity. Ethnologia Europaea 21:145–70.

Huseby-Darvas, Éva V. 1987. Elderly Women in a Hungarian Village. Journal of Cross-Cultural Gerontology 2:15–42.

———. 1996. "Feminism, the Murderer of Mothers": The Rise and Fall of Neo-nationalist Reconstruction of Gender in Hungary. *In* Women Out of Place, Brackette F. Williams, ed. pp. 161–85. New York: Routledge.

Jackson, Robert J. 1992. The Changing Conditions of European Security in the Post-Cold War Era. *In* Europe in Transition. Robert J. Jackson, ed. pp. 3–17. New York: Praeger.

Janos, Andrew C. 1982. The Politics of Backwardness in Hungary. Princeton: Princeton University Press.

Jászi, Oscar. 1961. The Dissolution of the Habsburg Monarchy. Chicago: University of Chicago Press.

Jávor, Kata. 1990. The Socialization of Boys Versus the Socialization of Girls: Dissimilar Gender Roles in Two Hungarian Villages. East European Quarterly 23(4):409–418.

Kis, Janos. 1989. Turning Point in Hungary. Dissent 36:235–41. Translated by Gabor Follimus.

Kisbán, Eszter. 1989. From Peasant Dish to National Symbol: An Early Deliberate Example. Ethnologia Europaea 19(1):95–102.

Kisimre, Ferenc. 1993. Szellemi Vérszerződést Kötött Szegeden a Világ Szittyasága [The Szittyas of the World Made a Spiritual Bloodpact in Szeged]. Délmagyarország 83(148):1,5. June 28.

Konstantinov, Yulian. 1996. Patterns of Reinterpretation: Trader-Tourism in the Balkans (Bulgaria) as a Picaresque Metaphorical Enactment of Post-Totalitarianism. American Ethnologist 23(4):762–82.

Koppány, György. 1999. Two-In-Hand Carriage Driving World Cup in Kecskemét. Travel: The Hungarian Travel Magazine, 1999–2000, p. 27.

Kulcsár, Rózsa. 1985. The Socioeconomic Conditions of Women in Hungary. In Women, State, and Party in Eastern Europe. Sharon L. Wolchik and Alfred G. Meyer, eds. pp. 195–213. Durham: Duke University Press.

Kürti, László. 1990. People vs. the State: Political Rituals in Contemporary Hungary. Anthropology Today 6(2):5–8.

–––––––. 1991. The Wingless Eros of Socialism: Nationalism and Sexuality in Hungary. Anthropological Quarterly 64(2):55–67.

Lampland, Martha. 1991. Pigs, Party Secretaries, and Private Lives in Hungary. American Ethnologist 18(3):459–79.

–––––––. 1994. Family Portraits: Gendered Images of the Nation in Nineteenth-Century Hungary. East European Politics and Societies 8(2):287–316.

Larrabee, Stephen. 1993. East European Security after the Cold War. Prepared for the Under Secretary of Defense for Policy. RAND National Defense Research Institute.

Laszlo, Leslie. 1983. Nationality and Religion in Hungary, 1867–1918. East European Quarterly 17(1):41–56.

Lawson, Trevor. 1994. Plotting the Landscape. Geographical Magazine 66(11):42–44.

Markus, Maria. 1982. Overt and Covert Modes of Legitimation in East European Societies. In Political Legitimation in Communist States. T. H. Rigby and Ferenc Fehér, eds. pp. 82–93. New York: St. Martin's Press.

Marx, Karl. 1977. Capital, vol. 1. New York: Vintage Books. Translated by Ben Fowkes.

McIntyre, Robert J. 1985. Demographic Policy and Sexual Equality: Value Conflicts and Policy Appraisal in Hungary and Romania. In Women, State, and Party in Eastern Europe. Sharon Wolchik and Alfred G. Meyer, eds. pp. 270–85. Durham, NC: Duke University Press.

Michta, Andrew. 1992. East Central Europe after the Warsaw Pact. New York: Greenwood Press.

Mucha, Janusz L. 1993. An Outsider's View of American Culture. In Distant Mirrors, Philip R. DeVita and James D. Armstrong, eds., pp. 21–28. Belmont, CA: Wadsworth Publishing.

Natadecha-Sponsel, Poranee. 1993. The Young, the Rich, and the Famous: Individualism as an American Cultural Value. In Distant Mirrors, Philip R. DeVita and James D. Armstrong, eds., pp. 46–53. Belmont, CA: Wadsworth Publishing.

Népszabadság. 1992. Két Vizsgálat Tükrében. Gondsorrend: Munkanélküliség, Megélhetés [Two Looks in His Mirror. Order of Concern: Unemployment, Subsistence]. April 7:1,6.

Ortner, Sherry. 1974. Is Female to Male as Nature is to Culture? *In* Woman, Culture and Society. Michelle Zimbalist Rosaldo and Louise Lamphere, eds. pp. 67–88. Stanford: Stanford University Press.

Rosenberg, George S. and Donald F. Anspach. 1973. Working Class Kinship. Lexington, MA: D.C. Heath and Co.

Rubin, Lillian Breslow. 1976. Worlds of Pain. New York: Basic Books.

Sahlins, Peter. 1989. Boundaries. Berkeley: University of California Press.

Sampson, Steven. 1991. Is There an Anthropology of Socialism? Anthropology Today 7(5):16–19.

Schöpflin, George, Rudolf Tőkés and Iván Völgyes. 1988. Leadership Change and Crisis in Hungary. Problems of Communism Sept.-Oct. 37:23–46.

Simai, Mihaly. 1992. Hungarian Problems. Government and Opposition 27(1):52–65.

Stack, Carol. 1974. All Our Kin. New York: Harper and Row.

Stark, David and László Bruszt. 1998. Postsocialist Pathways. New York: Cambridge University Press.

Stewart, Michael. 1993. Gypsies, the Work Ethic and Hungarian Socialism. *In* Socialism: Ideals, Ideologies and Local Practice, C. M. Hann, ed. pp. 187–203. London: Routledge.

Stone, Linda. 1998. Kinship and Gender. Boulder, CO: Westview Press.

Sugar, Peter F. 1969. External and Domestic Roots of Eastern European Nationalism. *In* Nationalism in Eastern Europe. Peter F. Sugar, Ivo J. Lederer, eds. pp. 3–54. Seattle: University of Washington Press.

Szelenyi, Ivan. 1990. Alternative Futures for Eastern Europe: The Case of Hungary. East European Politics and Societies 4(2):231–54.

———. 1992. Social and Political Landscape, Central Europe, Fall 1990. *In* Eastern Europe in Revolution. Ivo Banac, ed. pp. 225-41. Ithaca, NY: Cornell University Press.

Tausz, Katalin. 1990. The Case of Eastern Europe: Why Community Development Still has Yet to Find a Role in Hungary. Community Development Journal 25(4):300–6.

Thorpe, Harry. 1975. The Homely Allotment: From Rural Dole to Urban Amenity: A Neglected Aspect of Land Use. Geography 60(3):169–83.

Tismaneanu, Vladimir. 1992. Reinventing Politics. New York: The Free Press.

Todorova, Maria. 1997. Imagining the Balkans. New York: Oxford University Press.

Tóth, József. 1988. Urbanizáció az Alföldön. [Urbanization on the Great Hungarian Plain]. Budapest: Akadémiai Kiadó.

users.ox.ac.uk/~cees/others/reg_economics.html. Accessed on 10/23/00.

Van Hoorn, Judith L., Ákos Komlósi, Elzbieta Suchar and Doreen A. Samelson. 2000. Adolescent Development and Rapid Social Change: Perspectives from Eastern Europe. Albany: SUNY Press.

Vasary, Ildikó. 1987. Beyond the Plan: Social Change in a Hungarian Village. Boulder. CO: Westview Press.

———. 1989. 'The Sin of Transdanubia': The One-Child System in Rural Hungary. Continuity and Change 4(3):429–68.

———. 1990. Competing Paradigms: Peasant Farming and Collectivization in a Balaton Community. The Journal of Communist Studies 6(2):163–82.

Verdery, Katherine. 1991a. National Ideology Under Socialism. Berkeley: University of California Press.

———. 1991b. Theorizing Socialism: A Prologue to the 'Transition.' American Ethnologist 18(3):419–39.

———. 1992. The Etatization of Time in Socialist Romania. *In* The Politics of Time. Henry Rutz, ed. pp. 38–61. American Ethnological Society Number 5. Washington, D.C.: American Anthropological Association.

Völgyes, Iván. 1980. Economic Aspects of Rural Transformation in Eastern Europe. *In* The Process of Rural Transformation: Eastern Europe, Latin America and Australia. Iván Völgyes, Richard E. Lonsdale and William P. Avery, eds. pp. 89–127. New York: Pergamon Press.

———. 1985. Blue-collar Working Women and Poverty in Hungary. *In* Women, State, and Party in Eastern Europe. Sharon L. Wolchik and Alfred G. Meyer, eds. pp. 221–33. Durham, NC: Duke University Press.

Völgyes, Iván and Nancy Völgyes. 1977. The Liberated Female. Boulder, CO: Westview Press.

Wæver, Ole. 1993. Societal Security: The Concept. *In* Identity, Migration and the New Security Agenda in Europe. Ole Wæver, Barry Buzan, Morten Kelstrup and Pierre Lemaitre, eds. pp. 17–40. New York: St. Martin's Press.

Wedel, Janine. 1986. The Private Poland. New York: Facts On File Publications.

West, B. A. 2000. Segments of Self and Other: The Magyar Hungarian Case. National Identities 2(1):49–64.

West, Barbara A. 1994. The Danger is Everywhere! Discourse on Security in Post-Socialist Hungary. The Anthropology of East Europe Review 12(2):17–25.

———. 1997. Nation Under Siege, Bodies Under Siege: Security as a Gendered Category in Hungarian National Identity. Working Papers on Women in International Development #260. East Lansing, MI: Women and International Development Program, Michigan State University.

www.ems.psu.edu/~williams/states/hu.htm. Accessed on 10/23/00.

Study Guide

Prepared by Nancy Ries
Colgate University

With the end of Soviet power over Eastern Europe in the late 1980s, and the collapse of single-party, paternalistic, and often repressive socialist regimes, much has changed for the countries formerly in the Soviet bloc: Poland, Czechoslovakia (now the Czech Republic and Slovakia), Romania, Bulgaria, Albania, Yugoslavia (now broken into smaller republics after the brutal wars of the 1990s), and Hungary. Like their peers in the countries of the former Soviet Union, tens of millions of people have experienced vast political, economic, social, and cultural changes—sometimes for the better, but often for the worse. While these changes throughout Eastern and Central Europe and the Balkans have opened up myriad new opportunities for the more entrepreneurial and more powerful members of the population, they have also brought confusion, dislocation, and insecurity for a majority of citizens.

Barbara West's study depicts this experience of confusion and insecurity from close up, in the city of Szeged, Hungary, using the methods of ethnographic participant observation. West tries to understand, and help us to understand, what it feels like to live in a period of profound, sometimes shocking social transformation. Some of the things she found are not at all obvious from afar—i.e., from perspectives more common to political scientists and macro-economists who examine political and economic change through a broader but much more distant lens.

Opportunities for anthropologists to do such close fieldwork in Eastern Europe were somewhat more limited before the 1990s. The same political liberalization that opened up all of the countries of the former Soviet Empire to many new forms of trade with Europe, the U.S., and other parts of the capitalist world, and which has spurred an influx of tourism and popular culture, also has permitted anthropologists and other scholars to have much greater access to communities and cultures that they wish to study. Until the 1990s, doing fieldwork in the ways that West describes would have been impossible. People would have been afraid to speak with her as openly as they did, and her communication and travel would have been restricted by bureaucrats and officials. Although in postsocialist times, the anthropologist may find herself limited in new ways and constrained by new fears (her own and those of local people), nevertheless she makes good use of the greater openness that characterizes Hungary today.

As you read this book, try to pay attention to your own reactions and feelings about the society that you are encountering. How are your evaluations of the Hungarian experience depicted in this ethnography shaped by Cold-War-era dichotomies of East and West? What are your reactions to reading the personal stories and commentaries presented here? Do you find yourself negatively judging the patterns of people's lives—or sympathetic to their struggles and fears?

Chapter 1

1. What kinds of things did the new ethnographer learn in the cafe on her second day in Hungary? Why do you think she opens the book with this story? What does she accomplish by opening this way? Do you think it's effective? What kind of image of Hungary does it set in your head (pp. 1–2)?

2. West tells us (p. 3) that her primary research question is to understand what it means to be Hungarian just after the end of socialism. How does her acquaintance's response to West's experience in the cafe (p. 2) speak about "being Hungarian"?

3. The concept of "insecurity" is presented as a key framing element of Hungarian identity (p. 3). Does that seem strange to you? We are used to thinking about identity in relation to all sorts of things (cultural patterns, traditions, beliefs, aesthetics, and values) but usually not with reference to something like "insecurity." Would you say that by the end of this chapter West convinces us of the rich local meanings embedded in that concept? What does it seem to mean and why is it so important to being Hungarian in the early 1990s?

4. Why did Hungarians talk about being citizens of the "most comfortable barrack in the [Soviet] camp" (p. 4)? Is that meant to be humorous or serious?

5. Do you think that you would trade your "right to speak out" (p. 4) for day-to-day security in your life? Why/why not? What contexts of Hungarian history in the twentieth century might make this a widespread choice (i.e., why might many people choose material security over "freedom of speech")?

6. In 1956, Soviet army tanks rolled into Hungary and violently quashed a revolutionary uprising against Communist control. What is surprising about the revolution that took shape in 1989? What did it accomplish (pp. 5–6)?

7. How do the author's impressions of Hungary and of Szeged and its people differ from those of the people themselves (pp. 8–9)? Why do you think their views are different? Much (though not all) ethnography involves anthropologists studying "others"—people in communities sometimes vastly different from their own. What are the advantages of this "outsider perspective"? What are the disadvantages? Think about ways in which the disadvantages might be overcome through specific methods of ethnographic fieldwork and writing (pp. 11–13). How does West employ these?

8. West remarks that for Hungarians in Szeged "their social idiom was a security idiom" (p. 8). What does this mean? (What is a "social idiom"?) Do you think Szeged natives would talk about themselves this way? How does their use of the security idiom differ from those of political leaders (pp. 9–11)?

9. Ethnographic accounts often begin with a detailed description of the anthropologist's arrival in a new and unfamiliar place. What kinds of things do we learn from West's account? What is the mood she sets by telling the story of her arrival?

Chapter 2

1. Why does the author distinguish between "state" and "nation"? What are the key concepts linked to the idea of the Hungarian (Magyar) nation (pp. 19–20)?

2. Find maps of Hungary and Eastern Europe in your library or on the Internet. Locate Szeged on the map of Hungary and note all of the countries that border Hungary. What role does Hungary's geographical location and historical experience play in the construction of Hungarian identity today (pp. 20–26)?

3. What are some of the paradoxes and contradictions in gender relations over time in Hungary? Do you think that issues of gender are more of a national concern (or a concern of the state) in the U.S. or in Hungary? What do you see as key differences in gender relations and gender politics in Hungary and in the U.S. (pp. 25–29)?

4. Why is the concept of the nation important for the anthropologist to examine? What do people's ideas about their nationhood tell us about their culture?

Chapter 3

1. What surprises you in West's discussion of Christmas and friendship in Hungary (pp. 31–35)? Would things be different in the community or family in which you grew up? If you were the anthropologist, how would you have felt at being "left out" of most people's celebrations?

2. How do economic or material factors shape the ways in which Hungarians in Szeged regard their friends (pp. 35–41)? Why and in what ways has the ending of the socialist period affected their friendships? Can you think of any ways in which economic or political changes have affected your family's (nuclear or extended) patterns?

3. Why couldn't West's Hungarian acquaintances accept the idea of "potluck suppers" or her offers to contribute something to a meal? How did you feel about their reactions? What did you learn from them? What do the anecdotes on pp. 38 and 40 suggest about ways in which anthropologists learn about other cultures?

4. Do you sense that the people West spoke with about their families and relatives experience a sense of loss or longing for more active relationships with their kin (pp. 41–44)?

5. What are the main reasons people give for not celebrating traditional holidays like Christmas, the New Year, and Easter in any significant or collective ways (pp. 43–46)? What do you think would be the long-term and widespread consequences if the majority of people in your home community felt the same way? Do members of your own family ever use the same explanations for not making a big deal of major holidays or birthdays? What general contextual factors might help to explain the fervent energy many people in the U.S. put into holiday celebrations?

6. What does the contrast between people's seeming indifference to national holidays and their enthusiastic response to President Göncz's speech in Szeged in 1994 say about their general attitude towards the state, politics, and public life (pp. 46–49)?

7. Make a list of the different people you share food with on a regular basis (both at home and at college) and organize this list around different kinds of food events (homemade meals [large or small], "treating" in a restaurant, going out together but not treating, picnics, barbecues, weddings, etc.). Following the argument by Mary Douglas that West presents on p. 50, think about whether these different kinds of food-sharing practices delineate degrees of social "inclusion" and "exclusion" in your community of friends, relatives, family, etc.

8. Does it seem paradoxical to you that weddings (p. 51) are such complex and involving events, in contrast to holiday celebrations? How would you explain that contrast?

9. What do you make of the anecdotes that West tells about keys and dogs (pp. 52–54)? How does she analyze or interpret these stories in order to make sense of them? Can you think of any other interpretations?

Chapter 4

1. West argues that there is a strong connection between gardening activity and identity as Hungarian (pp. 57–60) and that people garden intensely not just for reasons of practical survival but also for reasons of symbolic cultural survival. What do you make of this argument? Can anything comparable be said about the cultural milieu in which you grew up? Do gardens or yards form a crucial part of people's identities in your community?

2. Read the four "Case Studies" (pp. 60–70) carefully. You may want to read them through twice. As you do, make a list of things you learn about Hungarian history, economy, society, people, family life, and culture from reading these stories. Think about the stories both individually and in relation to each other. Try to come up with at least twenty separate points. What do case studies such as these tell you as a reader that other forms of ethnographic representation cannot? What important things about culture can you *not* learn from these kinds of stories?

3. The author focuses on the question of how these individual case studies illustrate people's use of gardens as vehicles for enacting, imagin-

ing, or relating to "security" in today's Hungary (pp. 70–72). She also discusses the relationship of gardening and being part of an "imagined Hungarian community" (p. 73). Do you think anything else is going on? Can you construct alternative interpretations of what gardening means given the information available to you?

4. Mini-comparative project: Interview a few family members, friends, acquaintances, or people in the neighborhood where you live who are active gardeners. How would you get at what gardening "means" for them? Write up your own "case study" using the ones that West provides as models for what to include. How did your interviewees get into gardening? Where is their land in relation to their homes? What kinds of things do they grow and how do they use their produce? Does gardening provide a sense of security for them (symbolic or material) or a connection to an imagined American community? Does gardening form part of their personal or cultural identity? What does gardening mean for them? How would they feel if they couldn't garden?

Chapter 5

1. For what reasons does West decide to take this journey to Istanbul, despite what people have said about the dangers (pp. 75–77)? As you read to the end of the chapter, think about whether this trip was ethnographically useful to her, and if so, whether it was useful in the ways she anticipated before starting out.

2. What are shopper-traders? Why do they make this arduous journey to Turkey on a regular basis? Why didn't they help West and her friends out when extra money was demanded from them, on two occasions, at the Serbian border (pp. 80 and 85)? Do you think they were right or sensible not to help the U.S.-American anthropologist? Do you think she was right in not helping them, in turn (pp. 86–87)? How would you have behaved in these situations? What connections do you see between the events in this chapter and the issues of social relationships discussed in chapter 3?

3. What are the various meanings of "balkán" among Hungarians? Do you think West can fully escape adopting some of the local ethnocentrism that this term implies (p. 89)?

4. How important is the concept of "balkán" in constructions of Hungarianness? What is the polar opposite of that term (pp. 87–91)?

5. What feelings do you have when you read about the episodes at the end of this chapter pertaining to time and action (pp. 91–96)? Why were West's fellow travelers so reluctant to complain about delays, leave their group, or explore on their own? Can you think of reasons other than those which the author provides?

Chapter 6

1. West discusses the development of discourses about criminality and exhaustion in the early and mid-1990s (pp. 103–108). What does she mean by the concept of discourse? Are people's expressions of fear based on truly significant increases in crime, or are they exaggerations? Why do you think people are talking this way and feeling so afraid?

2. How do fears about local and personal safety reflect larger concerns about the Hungarian nation? What role does a changing economic situation play in all of this discourse?

3. West calls security discourse the "master narrative" of Szeged (p. 112). What does she mean by that? What happens when politicians begin to wield this narrative? Can you think of any comparable "master narratives" in your own society?

4. In what key ways is this chapter ethnographically different from the others in the book? What methods does West use in this chapter to record and report meaningful aspects of the lives of the people of Szeged? Would a political scientist be likely to write about Hungary in the same ways?

Chapter 7

1. For people of Szeged, what is the meaning of violent crimes against or harassment of Hungarian women perpetrated by "balkán" men (p. 119)? Why, according to West, do people choose this particular idiom through which to express their fears? Can you think of anything similar in your culture?

2. The constraints on and expectations of Hungarian women (pp. 123–129) may seem oppressive and old-fashioned to you. Do you get any sense that Hungarians perceive them that way? What factors may be necessary in a society to release people from such inflexible gender norms?

3. As West shows, ideas about gender intersect very profoundly with ideas about the health and security of the nation. Compare the "official" and "public" representations and uses of gender (pp. 129–132) with those of everyday life. Through what cultural mechanisms are these spheres related?

4. Does the discussion of gender in this chapter shed additional light on the findings about personal networks reported in chapter 3?

Chapter 8

1. What can we learn about the processes and practices of fieldwork by reading West's comparison of her experience in the early 1990s with that of her return trip in 1996?

2. Why is it useful for an ethnographer to return to the field site from time to time over a period of several years? What do we learn about Hungary and the postsocialist experience in general by thinking about the changes that took place between West's first and second visits?

3. How would you explain the very warm reception that the anthropologist received when she arrived in 1996, especially considering the revelations in chapter 3?

General Questions

1. Try to isolate some of the specific ethnographic methods that West used in her fieldwork. Overall, which of the methods for gathering and presenting her "data" did you find the most successful for conveying the lived experience of postsocialism in Szeged?

2. A fairly clear image of the ethnographer herself emerges through the course of this work. Why do you think West chose to tell stories the

way she did, so that her role in the events she describes is fairly clear to the reader? Does that ethnographic reflexivity help us understand Hungarian culture and society? How?

3. What does this book teach you about postsocialist countries in general? What does it say about the so-called "transition" to capitalism? Is the story about the postsocialist period in Hungary that this book tells different from what you might have expected when you started it? In what ways?

4. Having read this ethnography, explain why you think West focused on the idiom/concept of security. What does insecurity mean in Hungary at the present time?

5. Despite an atmosphere of loss, anxiety, and insecurity, there are aspects of life in Szeged that you might find appealing and fascinating. If you were planning an ethnographic field research project, what kinds of things might attract you to do a research project in Szeged or elsewhere in Hungary?